"Most businesses today are draining the life out of their most essential assets: their workers. Moe Carrick – with her brilliant new book *Bravespace Workplace* – will help us change this toxic paradigm. Warm, witty and data-driven, Carrick unflinchingly tackles the false dichotomy that a company must choose between profit and people. She shows us how to transform our workplace into a culture that brings out the best in our people. I am grateful for the opportunity to use Carrick's refreshing and practical Bravespace model with my team."

— **Glennon Doyle,** author of the #1 *New York Times* bestseller *Love Warrior* and founder of Together Rising

"Today more than ever, effective leadership requires more not just the head but the heart as well. In *Bravespace Workplace,* Moe Carrick outlines how leaders can strengthen their organizations through caring, connecting, and cultivating healthy cultures. This is a must read for leaders who want their people, and their organizations, to thrive."

— **Ron Fritz,** CEO, Tech Soft 3D

"*Bravespace Workplace* . . . a must read for today's leaders: When a workplace is toxic, then the employee's energy is spent 'coping,' with great cost in their happiness, health, and creativity. And there is great loss to the organization: through lost opportunity. In *Bravespace Workplace*, Moe Carrick shows how to diagnose key toxic issues, and how to engage to create an organization where 'humans can show up as they are.' Performance will soar!"

— **Rod Ray,** PhD, PE, founder and former CEO, Bend Research

"Moe Carrick understands the future of the workplace. Her open-hearted, trust-centric approach to business leadership is not only good for employees, but it's also good for the economy."

— **Vanessa Childers,** Editorial Director, Conscious Company Media

"Early on, we realized that culture is an enduring competitive advantage and our people have been key to Hydro Flask's success ever since. This book offers inspiration and practical tools for any employer who wants to win both by doing what is best for their people and subsequently winning the war for talent."

— **Scott Allan,** SVP and Global GM, Hydro Flask

"Moe Carrick does it again – her new book, *Bravespace Workplace*, is a must-read, especially for people leaders. Moe's lifelong work of studying work cultures and human performance are illuminated in her book. She has spent several decades studying how human's need a sense of purpose, to be seen, valued, and nurtured. She has witnessed, time and again, companies who foster cultures where these important dimensions exist in an authentic way, see it in both the bottom-line results of their organizations and in how customers are taken care of. She provides practical methods to chart your journey to enriching the lives of others and self along the way. A worthwhile read!"

— **Michelle Clemens,** Vice President of Human Resources, Seattle University

"In business? Then you're in the 'people business.' And if you're not creating, growing, and leading a Bravespace Workplace, you're at risk. This is the instruction manual you've been waiting for!"

— **David Taylor-Klaus,** PCC, CPCC, CTPC, CC-IQC, founder of DTK Coaching

"Moe captures a poignant message that has never been more important for our humanity and the future of work: How do we bring our best whole-selves to every part of our lives – including work where we spend the majority of waking hours? Her transparent and vulnerable voice is easy to read, easy to love and an *inspiring* call to action for all stakeholders in the global economy. A must-read for aspiring world-changers like me bucking the status quo!"

— **Shannon Keith,** CEO and Founder of Sudara

"As leaders we need to value the human spirit, the unique contributions that individually we bring to a company. These unique voices, ideas, energies coming together gives us strength. In *Bravespace Workplace* Moe Carrick offers tools and inspiration to help guide leaders who want to apply a conscious culture and create a company where everyone can thrive. How impactful to have everyone know they are a valued part of your organization and able to contribute at their highest and best level!"

— **Kathy Kull,** Corporate Director Human Resources, Blommer Chocolate

"*Bravespace Workplace* offers practical tools and necessary inspiration for leaders about creating an environment where their people can thrive, be joyful, and feel that their opinions and contributions matter."

— **Marc Hoffman,** Partner, A.T. Kearney

"It seems so simple, remembering to lead with heart. *Bravespace Workplace* gave me thoughtful questions to ask myself on how to lead to ensure our business is people and planet first."

— **Casey Hanisko,** President, ATTA / Adventure 360

"A company's biggest asset is its human capital. So why do so many squander it with one-size-fits-all policies and neglectful practices? Creating a worker-centered workplace is not only the right thing to do, it's good business. And this book is your blueprint, a must for every leader and manager."

— **Norie Quintos,** principal at Norie Quintos Media and editor at large at *National Geographic Traveler*

"This book provides practical, easy to implement tools to do right by those in your workplace, and in doing so, to ensure that your business does well, and the world does better. Thank you Moe Carrick!"

— **Mara Rudman,** JD, Senior VP Policy/Projects, Business Executives for National Security; former Deputy Assistant to the President, National Security Council

"Business owners and CEOs are still designing workplaces and company cultures in antiquated ways. It's no surprise that the youth of today are shying away from corporate jobs, even vilifying them. They simply leave no space for individuality and they don't ask themselves often enough, what can we do for our people. This book is a daring and refreshing manuscript on how to break this mold and re-invent company culture. We should all be inspired going to work every day and we should feel that the places we work are extensions of our value system. After all, we can accomplish so much more working together."

— **Omar Samra,** CEO, adventurer, and UN Goodwill Ambassador

"I am a firm believer that companies can win doing the right thing for the customer, employee, and shareholder. Too often companies favor the latter and the employee suffers the most. Moe offers a great handbook for managers to use to create a work environment for their teams to thrive and change the current paradigm."

— **Libby Unger,** Managing Director, Lumineau

"This is a book about how to disrupt how we think about work and work environments. Through an engaging, actionable blend of research and experience, *Bravespace Workplace* provides the vision and tools to create whole-hearted work environments where all are able to thrive. A practical, insightful guide for courageous leaders everywhere!"

— **Katie Kilty,** EdD, Principal, MindPower Resources

"There are now three billion working people on this planet. Forty percent of them report being happy, and thirteen percent are engaged at work. Highly diverse and inclusive workforces that are managed well, capture 46 to 58 percent higher financial performance. Being people-centric, *Bravespace Workplace* points out the way to make your people more happy and engaged."

— **Karen Brown,** Founder/Managing Director/Consultant, Bridge Arrow

"'People are messy.' After running businesses for nearly 40 years I was hit in the face like a wet fish by Moe's statement in *Bravespace*, and I'm grateful that it did.

— **Nicky Fitzgerald,** Founder and CEO, Angama Mara

"For anyone who has ever worked in a toxic environment and who says "Never again!" to that – read and share this book. We would have a happier and more fulfilled society if this was required reading (an enacting) for all CEOs."

— **Daniela Papi-Thornton,** CEO, Systems-led Leadership

"As a community leader, I strongly believe in finding common ground, shared values, and genuinely safe spaces where individuals can thrive and are inspired to work together for the greater good. Carrick's *Bravespace Workplace* is the perfect guide for creating that positive, healthy, and highly functioning workplace the world needs more of."

— **Sally Russell,** Mayor, Bend, Oregon

"Carrick's new book is inviting and provocative. She understands what it takes to create healthy workplaces – Bravespaces – and offers a workable model and practical behaviors we can employ right now to make them a reality."

— **Judy Ringer,** author of *Turn Enemies into Allies: The Art of Peace in the Workplace*

"Every business professional will benefit from this essential reading (on work in the 21st century). Moe Carrick will inspire you to rethink everything you thought you knew about the workplace and provides honest, clear-eyed, and healing recommendations for our best work-lives."

— **Laura Wendt,** PhD, neuroscientist, international speaker, and Manager, Global Diversity and Inclusion, at A.T. Kearney

"In a day and age where businesses range from megacorporate America to your one-person start-ups, Moe Carrick has a way to relate to every human being weathering the highs and lows of their careers with wisdom, experience, and, most importantly, heart. Moe not only presents a broad perspective on how to maneuver your career but also adds tools and techniques to become more successful professionally and personally. *Bravespace Workplace* is a must-read for anyone looking to grow their business and their own capacity for success."

— **Molly Carroll,** therapist, speaker, and author of *Cracking Open* and *Trust Within: Letting Intuition Lead*

"As a pioneering organization operating in two post-conflict countries with staff from many different ethnic backgrounds, we have faced many challenges working together. In *Bravespace Workplace* Moe Carrick offers a roadmap for leaders everywhere for what really matters in their roles.

— **Praveen Moman,** Founder and CEO, Volcanoes Safaris (Uganda/Rwanda)

"Moe's passion is strewn throughout these stories, her experiences, and this guidebook for brave, better workplaces. Simple but not easy, clear but not directive, Moe unpacks the heart and bits of healthy work worlds."

— **Christine Olex,** Owner, The Point

"In today's healthcare environment, creating a Bravespace Workplace is an amazing opportunity to counteract the impact of the complexity and uncertainty that underlies the current system."

— **Megan Haase,** FNP, CEO Mosaic Medical

BRAVESPACE WORKPLACE

BRAVESPACE WORKPLACE

Making Your Company
Fit for Human Life

MOE CARRICK

MAVEN HOUSE

Published by Maven House Press, 4 Snead Ct., Palmyra, VA 22963
610.883.7988 • www.mavenhousepress.com.

Special discounts on bulk quantities of Maven House Press books are available to corporations, professional associations, and other organizations. For details contact the publisher.

For information about subsidiary rights (translation, audio, book club, serial, etc.) contact rights@mavenhousepress.com.

While this publication is designed to provide accurate and authoritative information in regard to the subject matter covered, it is sold with the understanding that the publisher is not engaged in rendering legal, accounting, or other professional service. If legal advice or other expert assistance is required, the services of a competent professional person should be sought. — From the Declaration of Principles jointly adopted by a Committee of the American Bar Association and a Committee of Publishers and Associations

Library of Congress Control Number: 2018968332

Paperback ISBN: 9781938548437
E-book ISBN: 9781938548444

Printed in the United States of America.

Dedication

≈

THIS BOOK IS DEDICATED TO WORKERS EVERYWHERE, the employees at the front line who do the things that must be done at workplaces large and small. You are the heart of it all, and it's what you do every day that makes your company great. Remember that work is important to life, and the two are intertwined. Hold fast to being brave, even when it feels hard, because bringing your whole self to work matters.

And to the people leaders out there – you are central to Bravespace workplaces. People know their organization through you, and their entire experience is shaped by their relationship with you. Remember that, more than anything else, people need and want you to show up authentically with both your gifts and your flaws. You are enough.

Contents

෨

Foreword

꙰

I WENT TO HARVARD BUSINESS SCHOOL in the late 80s. We were taught that leaders were strong and decisive. That they dressed and spoke with confidence and knew how to work a room to achieve their goals. We were taught to be rigorous with our analysis and to always deliver on our commitments. We learned how to navigate financial statements and organizational charts and marketing plans. I remember so many cases and courses and discussions about how to be successful, but I don't remember a single conversation about how or why I might need to be brave.

With the perspective of time, however, I see that many of my best moments as an employee and as a leader involved courage. Courage required me to push beyond my comfort zone – taking an assignment I wasn't fully prepared for, or deviating from the typical linear career path. Stepping away from a cushy headquarters job to go out to the field and sell. Moving my family across the country for a radical career change. Letting go of a high-performing employee who was creating a toxic work environment. These decisions all took courage. And while they didn't all go as planned, each brave decision showed me the value of navigating by my own success criteria and not by conventional wisdom.

Sometimes bravery involved speaking truth to power, which was especially challenging as a female leader in male-dominated situations.

Many times bravery involved how I showed up for my team. Learning the paradox of confidence and humility required me to admit when I didn't know the answer or had made a mistake. Learning that great teams happen when I hire people who are better than me, not people I can control. Having the difficult conversations that require both radical candor and care when someone isn't performing or is in the wrong job.

It's hard work to be a brave leader. I have failed more times than I have succeeded. It's so much easier to retreat behind your spreadsheet than to dive into the messy, difficult business of people's hearts. In fact, early in my career I took a Myers-Briggs personality assessment that pegged me as a natural Feeler (F) who had trained herself to be a Thinker (T). The coach counseled that that's a difficult place to be –to know that many work situations require you to lead with objectivity and rationality, and to prioritize logic over emotions, while at heart being deeply empathetic to the human factors involved in decisions. At the time I dismissed her comments and took pride in the fact that I had learned to shape myself in the mold of the more typical business leader.

Now I see it differently. The world needs brave leaders who understand that bringing their heart to work doesn't mean they're weak, or don't care about results, or don't have what it takes to make tough decisions.

As Moe points out, "People are what make companies great," and employees today have more choices than ever – f they don't like their boss or their work environment, they'll leave to find another. And even if they don't leave, they surely won't give their full effort to an employer that they see as unaware or unempathetic to the realities of life's messiness. As leaders, how do we create an environment where employees can thrive and contribute fully to the success of their organizations?

Simply put, we must commit to creating the conditions that allow employees to bring their best selves to work. We can pursue what Moe calls Bravespace workplaces. For the young manager this might mean taking the time to get to know her direct reports and being honest about her own limitations and fears. (I still remember how demoralized I was by a first-time boss who felt that she needed to assert her power by micromanaging me, even though she only had one more year of experience than me.) For the head of a department, it might mean actively creating a shared sense of purpose by thinking as deeply about the team dynamics as he does about managing each individual. For an executive it might mean boldly pursuing policies such as flexible work hours or paternity leave to help reduce employees' stress stemming from family commitments.

As leaders, we each have the opportunity and responsibility to show up with courage and conviction. We each have the opportunity to develop both the heart and the head that we bring to our work.

When I reflect on the leaders who have drawn out my best work, I realize that they're the ones who have shown me that I was seen and cared for. They didn't shy away from giving me tough feedback, and they certainly didn't accept shoddy efforts or poor results. But those actions aren't the ones that carried the biggest impact. What I hold sacred is the memory of the boss who flew across the country to attend my Dad's funeral. The boss who bought me a bottle of champagne when I completed a particularly onerous project. The boss who said yes to a part-time arrangement when I wanted to help my husband start a business. These actions brought out my best self. These leaders taught me to be brave.

I am fortunate that what I didn't learn about courage and heart from business school I was able to learn from these wise bosses and from my own successes and failures. But I so wish I had had Moe's book.

I'm envious of the young manager about to dive into the pages ahead. You can learn so much that will positively impact you and the people you'll go on to lead. I feel kinship with those of you of my vintage. Our age frees us from some of the fears about our own careers and gives us the opportunity to speak up about what we believe to be right.

Moe's book gives us data and techniques that we can use to positively change broken systems.

Together we can change workplaces and make them actually work for the people who inhabit them. Together we can create the bravespaces that will improve our businesses, our communities, and the world.

Cammie Dunaway
CMO, Duolingo

Acknowledgments

༄

THE EXPERIENCE OF WORKING WITH CLIENTS these past 30 years is at the core of my learning, and I'm grateful and humbled by the privilege of working with every single one of you. You have opened your companies to me, invited me into your innermost fears, and shared your legacy dreams. It's a privilege and an honor to work beside you. Globally, hundreds of thousands of employees come to work day in and day out counting on you to provide good work for them, to help them grow, and to enable the health and success of their families and communities. Watching you be brave as you lead your organizations gives me hope for our collective future. Thank you.

I appreciate the social justice and education leaders (Brian Arao and Kristi Clemens, Diana Ali, et al.) who first coined the term *bravespace* as an alternative to *safe space* when describing the way college campuses protect and support freedom of expression. I had used the term *bravespace* to define the workplaces I felt were necessary in business tomorrow before I learned of the term's use in the university context, and while the context is different for Bravespace workplaces, the meaning is adjacent and aligned. Thank you for your work.

Huge shout-outs to my publisher Jim Pennypacker (Maven House Press) and my agent Kelli Christianson for your unwavering faith in me, your patience, your honest feedback, and the delight of partnership. To my editor Cameron Carrick, your critical eye, challenging questions, endless compassion, and inquisitive mind were assets in every stage of writing, especially the last one, where we wrestled the book down to its essence.

To my family and friends, thank you for understanding and patiently loving me through research, writer's block, editing binges, and self-criticism, even while I missed precious time with you in order to birth *Bravespace Workplace*. Thank you to my children, Ian, Cam, and Hannah Carrick and Jesse Morris and Barb Lish – the future is in good hands with you and you inspire me so. Mom, thanks for just always. To my dear friends Ann Lent, Sandy Corbari, and Dana Rhode, you always have my back and have kept me going on some dark days of doubt. You are my why. Mei Ratz – your partnership caught me by surprise and has been a gift beyond measure. Your contributions every step of the way to this book and in our work are enlivening and immeasurable.

And to Jim – my person – I am the luckiest woman to be loved by you.

Prologue

❧

MY FATHER WAS THE ARCHETYPE OF THE ARTIST: brilliant, handsome, cash-deficient, and prone to over-drinking. When I was six, he wrapped a car around a pole, attended an Alcoholics Anonymous meeting, and began his journey to sobriety. Over the next decade, when I visited my Dad, my siblings and I sat in on many of these AA meetings. As I grew up, they were the closest thing I had to church. We went regularly (and mostly enjoyed the donuts), and my Dad found his people there. What's more, everyone in those halls had the same focus: just for today, let's not drink. It was a simple but often very challenging goal whose consequences radiated out into each member's broader community. I learned a lot from sitting in on these meetings. Most of all, I learned what it means to be brave.

There was a shared understanding that each person's sobriety was their own responsibility and that the others would wholly support those present. Whether twenty years sober or a day away from the last binge, people were encouraged and expected to be honest. Over and over, I saw the courage that people needed to admit their failures and strive to create for themselves a better world. This was work, and it was challenging, ragged, and rewarding.

Today I work as a consultant to organizations. I help people in workplaces meet their goals, whether to make a profit or achieve a mission. Organizations call me for culture and people issues. With hindsight, looking back over the course of my career, I can see a theme common to those meetings of my youth and the work environments my clients try to create: both are places where individuals are encouraged to bring their honest selves, challenged to meet the goals they have set, and supported by their community. I call these companies, the ones that engage their people, elevate the practice of leadership, and model healthy cultures as a practice of meeting their goals, Bravespace workplaces. These employers activate, enliven, and tenderly support the complex and vulnerable humans we are when we're at work, so that we can bring all our talent, creativity, and energy to work every day.

This book is a call to action and an instruction guide for business owners, entrepreneurs, CEOs, board members, HR personnel, leaders at every level, and employees to create workplaces in all sectors that are brave enough to operate, day in and day out, in ways that bring out the best in the people who work there.

My motivation to write *Bravespace Workplace* comes from my experiences, over the past 30 years, in helping hundreds of organizations of all kinds to achieve their goals.

In my work I've seen some organizations that shine. In these companies, employees enjoy coming to work because they're appreciated for what they bring in all forms and employers are happy with the achievements of their organization because their people play an active role in the results. More commonly, though, I encounter toxic workplaces. Toxic workplaces hurt. People who work in toxic environments are often demoralized, unengaged, stressed, anxious, scared, and dissatisfied. Their work consists of doing time, serving a sentence, of sorts, to get by, but most certainly these people are not thriving. I'm tired of seeing workplaces that are inhospitable to the human beings who work in them.

On the one hand, I get it. In today's world we trade our time for the money that buys the things that sustain and entertain us – housing, food, commodities. Consider, though, that most full-time workers spend most of their lives working. What are the consequences of looking at work as a prison sentence? Is work only a direct trade for money?

Toxic workplaces have myriad consequences – on profit, on the planet, and on people.

Research shows how people are doing in the modern workplace – and most people around the world report feeling underutilized, unhappy, unengaged, and dissatisfied at work. If spending your life in this state isn't bad enough, consider that, as Stanford professor Jeffry Pfeffer (2018) says in his book *Dying for a Paycheck*, "more deaths [come] from poor, unhealthful, stressful workplace conditions than the number of deaths resulting from diabetes, Alzheimer's, influenza, or kidney disease and about as many deaths as were reported in 2010 from both accidents and strokes." Work is not only draining the life out of us, but in many ways, it is killing us.

Profit is the main reason that most companies exist. A necessary element in our global economy, when profit is pursued single-mindedly as the only goal, the consequences are often disasterous for people in the workplace as well as for the environment and the communities in which businesses operate. The relentless pressure that publicly held companies endure from their shareholders to increase profits, quarter after quarter, creates untenable choices for leaders. I argue that everyone, in every business, must focus beyond the organization's short-term profitability. It matters, but it is not the *only* thing that matters. People are at the very root of what makes organizations great, in every sector. It's time to stop expecting employees to heroically serve their companies as if their very lives depend on it, and instead look toward creating workplaces perfectly suited for people.

In Chapters 1–3, I examine what makes companies "healthy" and explore the effects of business on the health of our communities and our environment. I also tackle a salient issue of our time: technology. Technology is an ever-present enabler of transaction speed, data analysis, and insight, and in recent years it has added complexities

"

Toxic workplaces have myriad consequences – on profit, on the planet, and on people.

to the work of people. I explore these complexities, proposing a shift in our mindset away from fear of technology and toward viewing it as a tool that can enable companies to bring out in their employees the best and most uniquely human traits for a better future. In my view, profit and technology must be considered in the context of ensuring that work and workplaces are fit for human life, now and in the future.

For most leaders, the hard parts of their role are not the nuances of designing their product, understanding their financials, or ensuring capital for expansion. What I've seen, consistently, is that what frustrates and fatigues good leaders, and causes them to falter, are the complexities, idiosyncrasies, and consequences of the very human nature of their most essential asset: the people who work for them. In Chapters 4–6, I address this frustration by explaining, in detail, what makes some workplaces toxic and unhealthy for some people. I explore the basics that we need from work and propose a new definition of a great workplace – a Bravespace workplace – that meets people's needs so that they can support the goals of the organization where they work.

"

What I've seen, consistently,
is that what frustrates and
fatigues good leaders, and
causes them to falter, are the
complexities, idiosyncrasies,
and consequences of the very
human nature of their most
essential asset: the people
who work for them.

In Chapters 7–11, I offer solutions for transforming organizations of all kinds into Bravespace workplaces, where people can show up as they are, both worthy and flawed, and do great things together. We can bring the entirety of ourselves to work every day in Bravespace workplaces. Creating Bravespace workplaces requires looking closely at how we lead, how we collaborate, and how we design our workspaces, our interactions, and the work itself. These chapters follow a Who-What-Where/When-Why-How format to help readers connect to five essential levers for success in transforming their organizations so that they're fit for human life.

Finally, Chapter 12 is a call to action. It offers ten practical behaviors that you can begin to employ right now to make your company a Bravespace workplace. Doing so will activate the best that your people have to bring to their work, benefitting your company's results, its bottom line, the communities in which it operates, the environment it requires, and the value that it adds.

When human beings bring their best to work every day, it's good for the organization they work for because it helps the organization make a profit and meet its mission. When organizations succeed, they contribute to the fabric of global social and economic interdependencies that our survival as a species depends upon. The war for talent, the rise of machines and artificial intelligence as partners at work, and the nature of our interconnected global economy demand that every organization fosters health for the people who work there.

It's time to stop letting profit delude us into thinking that profit is singularly enough. I'm heartsick seeing leaders in business know what to do and not doing it – we have known what it takes to create human-hospitable workplaces for most of my adult life. People are what make companies great, and the world has big problems that need great companies to solve them. There is a better way to run a business. Let's explore how.

"

Creating Bravespace workplaces requires looking closely at how we lead, how we collaborate, and how we design our workspaces, our interactions, and the work itself.

PART I

❧

People Make Companies Great

Chapter 1

~

The Messy Details of
Defining *Great*

To define is to limit.

— Oscar Wilde, *The Picture of Dorian Gray*

ON SOME DAYS I'VE LOVED GOING TO WORK. Like the day I got to commute on my bike through the Italian countryside, where I worked with a terrific family-held business that sought, successfully, to strengthen its team; or when I worked as a clinical counselor, and a patient was making a breakthrough, knew it, and shared out loud her appreciation for my work, saying it made a difference; or the hot summer days in my teens when, in a local ice-cream shop, I made summertime feel festive for our entire community. I even loved the time my boss and I spent all night in a Kinko's, me with my breastfeeding baby in tow, refining our materials for a client gig the following day.

While I'm fortunate to have had these work experiences, they haven't all been treasured. Some of my work experiences have been quite unpleasant: a few boring, some even hopeless, where I felt unseen, unimportant, or defeated. But over the course of my career I've often known that my work was making a difference, that what I did was good for someone, and that I was part of a team doing the thing that needed to be done. I know that, because of these experiences, I'm one of the lucky ones.

The thousands of people I've met as a consultant have shown me how lucky I've been. Sadly, I've heard story after story of folks who've struggled with boredom, isolation, stress, intimidation, fear, and frustration at work. That's why my work now consists of helping organizations find the right mix of actions and strategies that will activate the talents of their people so that they can achieve success.

I'm constantly thinking about how and why employees thrive and what makes a leader worth following. I notice the cacophony of voices in this field. I notice the thousands of business books published monthly. I notice the over 600,000 management consultants registered in the United States in 2017, and not just because I compete with them. The business magazines and publications that cloud our airplane reading, mailboxes, and digital spheres – *Bloomberg, Fast Company, Inc., Fortune*, etc. – often focus on one question: "What makes a company successful (aka 'great')?"

For more than 150 years our entire commerce system has answered this question with one word: *PROFIT*. Companies have historically focused on the increase in the gap between income and spending over time. As University of

Chicago professor Jonathan Levy (2014) says, while profit hasn't always meant the same thing, it always implies growth over time, often incessant growth. The economic models we've inherited are outdated. As British economist Kate Raworth (2017) says, "The citizens of 2050 are being taught an economic mindset that is rooted in the textbooks of 1950, which in turn are based on the theories of 1850." Relentless focus on quarter-over-quarter, year-over-year growth has had dire consequences.

First and foremost, we now live on a planet deeply scarred by our use of natural resources, and climate change is rapidly affecting production, resources, and economies (Pachauri and Meyer 2014). Second, we're seeing a staggering accumulation and concentration of wealth by a select few shareholders, resulting in wage stagnation and a crippling wage gap (Bloomberg 2018). Third, employees are more and more seeking purpose and meaning at work and are looking for ways to have a life and a lifestyle that works for them and their families (Gallup 2017b). Because of these changes, the conversations around how we work and what makes a company great are changing.

Employees are asking questions such as: "Does this job offer monetary compensation enough to cover the expenses of my lifestyle?" "Is there room for my personal development?" "Do my values and priorities match those of my workplace?" Companies listed in *Fortune* magazine's annual *100 Best Companies to Work For* and the *Great Place to Work* surveys boast benefits such as dedicated mindfulness rooms, healthy company culture, or "family" vibes. Their advertised assets point to the notion that employees today seek much more from work than the exchange of time for money.

Much of the media's attention about the modern workplace is focused on large public companies, especially the mega-tech companies Apple, Facebook, Google, and Amazon. These are often looked to as examples of how to organize people, what perks and benefits to offer employees, and best practices for management and culture. Yet, despite the concentration of wealth in companies like these, small businesses – defined as having fewer than 500 employees – still represent 99.7 percent of employer firms in the United States (Small Business Administration 2012).

Most of us work for small businesses, yet the conversations about great places to work focus on mega-corporate America. What this means is that the real variation in great places to work goes unrecognized in popular media outlets. People are miserable in both large and small workplaces, but people often think about big companies when it comes to workplace health and culture because that's what we see in popular media.

But small organizations play a gigantic role in how we work, and they also have some advantages when it comes to being fit for human life. *Small Giants* by *Inc.* editor Bo Burlingham (2016) highlights some of these advantages, including:

- The ability to change more quickly and more often

- The flexibility to customize solutions

- The ability (in private companies) to make investments and plan without having to report monthly profitability to Wall Street (protecting gross margins without compromising values)

- A strong focus on purpose as a driver

- Leadership deeply rooted in practical values

- Strong community connections and relationships

- Easier-to-cultivate meaningful relationships with customers, suppliers, employees, and stakeholders

In this book I discuss practices in all size organizations, but I'll focus on concepts, ideas, and tools to help leaders in small to mid-sized companies transform their organizations into brave, people-centered workplaces to achieve the results they seek. Of course, the concepts, ideas, and tools that I describe in *Bravespace Workplace* are certainly relevant to large or mega corporations and will work there, but my emphasis is mostly on helping smaller organizations.

I spend my days asking people what elements make their work dreadful and what brings them personal fulfillment and engagement. The answers I get are personal and specific. As my co-author Cammie Dunaway and I wrote in

"

We human beings want all the things that make up a good life: love, play, challenge, community, giving back, freedom, safety, celebration, comfort, and health.

Fit Matters: How to Love Your Job (Carrick and Dunaway 2017), the process of defining *great* is more about determining the right place *for you* than it is a general assessment of greatness. Work fit (which is distinctly different from "fitting in") isn't easy to come by, and it requires solutions that are unique for each person.

There are some general features that people everywhere need. We human beings want all the things that make up a good life: love, play, challenge, community, giving back, freedom, safety, celebration, comfort, and health. We need the ability to support ourselves, to contribute, and to believe that what we do makes a difference to someone. People define *great* in a whole host of different ways, many of them highly personal. "Can I flex my hours to meet my personal needs?" "Is my commute to work long?" "Do I like my coworkers?" "Do I think my employer is paying me fairly?" "Am I the only one of me (black, gay, disabled, etc.)?"

In general, these questions aren't being asked often or early enough. According to the latest Conference Board job satisfaction survey, fewer than half of U.S. workers are satisfied with their jobs (Kan et al. 2018). Gallup (2017b) reports that 87 percent of employees worldwide are not engaged at work. What I see in my own work is that, unfortunately, many people give up their pursuit of a well-fitting job, persuaded by the belief that work is just a necessary evil, something you have to do to pay the bills. This apathy leads to misery, lost time, lost energy, and lost money.

We humans work a lot. And our culture of 24/7 digital connection, urgency, and immediacy means that, regardless of how many hours we formally work each week, people everywhere report that they're overwhelmed. For some it's the grueling demands of a professional role that knows no boundaries in terms of when we're on or off. For others it's the relentlessness of working two or three or four different jobs to cobble together enough money to support a family, leaving precious little time for anything but work. Although the Bureau of Labor Statistics (2018) says that the average American full-time worker over age 16 works 34.5 hours a week, most people, when you ask them, report that they think they work much more or "all the time." As journalist Brigid Schulte (2014) says in her bestselling book *Overwhelmed: Work, Love, and Play When No One Has the Time*, "Our perception of time is indeed our reality."

We spend more time at work than we do sleeping, eating, playing, or with family and friends (Smith Major et al. 2002). It's clear that life is too short for our work hours to be wasted in misery.

So What Do We Really Need?

For most of us, a great many of our needs are met by our workplaces, so happiness in life is strongly correlated to happiness in work. We crave being connected to others, contributing to something meaningful beyond self, and adding value to something that matters. When you feel good at work, you have energy and the capacity for creativity and partnership. This, in turn, creates a virtuous cycle in which the better you feel, the more you contribute at work. People are drawn to you in partnership and you get things done well with others.

People are not machines. Since we're human, it's important to our very survival that we add value and find purpose at work. Psychologist Abraham Maslow (1943) places meaningful work (as connected to self-esteem and self-actualization) in a critical spot in his hierarchy of needs for our human thriving: right behind physiological and safety

"

It's clear that life is too short for our work hours to be wasted in misery.

❝
People are not machines.

needs. As author and professor Barry Schwartz (2015) said in his book *Why We Work*, "To be satisfied with our work, we typically need a belief in the purpose of what we do."

And although Maslow placed the need for social connection behind physiological and safety needs, current theorists such as social research professor Brené Brown (2012) place the need for human beings to connect with other human beings on a par with the need for food, water, safety, and security. Connecting with people is necessary for our survival.

To illustrate this point, I'll tell you about a client of mine. This client operated in a large urban area and was involved in hosting a fair for homeless people during which they offered free services such as dental services, immunizations, food, housing vouchers, job support, etc. During the event, employees interacted with the city's homeless for the whole day. One employee was asked to survey attendees about what brought them out each year to the event – what did they most value. The single most important reason that people flocked to the event year after year was to connect with other people, to reduce the isolation and loneliness of living on the streets. The employee doing these interviews recommended that the firm spend less on offering stuff to the city's homeless and instead find ways to broker

"

We bring our very human need to connect with other people right smack dab into our jobs and our workplaces.

relationships between the attendees and the people providing the needed services.

We bring our very human need to connect with other people right smack dab into our jobs and our workplaces. Countless times, when I'm asked to support a client for culture development, team health, or leadership effectiveness, I find that the central problem is that employees are feeling unseen, alone, and unsupported at work. As Patrick Lencioni (2002), blockbuster author on teams and organizations, says, "More than anything else at work, people crave being seen, valued, and feeling like they contribute to work that matters (in any role at any level)."

Based on my experience with hundreds of organizations, thousands of individuals, and countless examples of both workplace misery and workplace thriving, combined with the astoundingly good research of others about organizational effectiveness and leadership impact, I have developed a short list of the needs that work should fulfill for us as human beings. Fulfilling these seven needs will facilitate the extent to which every one of us can bring ᴏᴜ. best ideas, our fullest energy, and our hardest effort to our work (drum roll please):

Seven Needs that Work Should Fulfill

- To meet our basic requirements – to make enough money or non-cash compensation to provide food, clothing, shelter, and safety

- To contribute – to do something that matters to someone

- To be seen – and known

- To connect – in real ways, with other people

- To learn – and become better

- To feel supported – to be able to be brave knowing that there are risks

- To make our lives work – to be able to do the things that matter to us and are ours to do

When we have these ingredients at work, we can bring our best to it, in the fullest sense. My most cherished work memories are the moments when the gifts that I had were perfectly suited to the problem and situation I faced *and* I was able to bring my full self to it. In those moments I felt brave, and even when I was extremely frightened, I could do the hard thing.

"

What makes an organization great? Being fit for the human beings who make it great and being designed purposefully to be so. Great organizations are employers that consciously and proactively invest time, energy, and resources to make their organizations Bravespace workplaces, where people can show up as they are, both worthy and flawed, and do great things together. Bravespace workplaces activate, enliven, and tenderly support the complex humans that we are so that we can bring our complete selves to work every day.

What makes an organization great? Being fit for the human beings who make it great and being designed purposefully to be so. Great organizations are employers that consciously and proactively invest time, energy, and resources to make their organizations Bravespace workplaces, where people can show up as they are, both worthy and flawed, and do great things together. Bravespace workplaces activate, enliven, and tenderly support the complex humans that we are so that we can bring our complete selves to work every day.

Working with this definition, in Chapter 2 let's explore the role that machines and artificial intelligence play in how we think about workplaces that are fit for human life.

Chapter 2

ﻬ

AI, Machines, and Robots, Oh My!

*In a properly automated and educated world, then,
machines may prove to be the true humanizing
influence. It may be that machines will do the work
that makes life possible and that human beings will
do all the other things that make life pleasant and
worthwhile.*

— Isaac Asimov, *Robot Visions*

IN MY FIRST JOB AFTER GRAD SCHOOL, the CEO of my
company, Craig McCaw, a leader in the burgeoning cel-
lular (before digital!) revolution, held an all-employee meeting and said that he believed that one day we would do
everything from our phones: banking, email, movies, route-
finding. Everything. He went on to say that someday we might
not even need the phones because we would have implants
in our heads that did it all. Frankly, we, the lowly workers,
thought that he was out of his mind. We had just gotten used
to the idea that our phones didn't need to be plugged into the

wall, and anyone wanting a "cell" phone was stuck carrying around a chunk of plastic the size of a bunch of celery.

But look at us now. Over three-quarters of the U.S. population own smartphones (Pew Research Center 2018). I use What's App to talk to my daughter in Buenos Aries. I order take-out, schedule the dog groomer, order meal tickets, plan my vacation, and look for an exercise class on this little device. Despite the challenges of the profit-based capitalist consumerist culture we live in that I mentioned in Chapter 1, we have this culture to thank for the development and mass production of our cherished devices. The world of work is full of paradoxes.

As most of us know, technological advances are speeding up. Many experts say that the issue is not whether technology will *speed* up, but rather whether we human beings will *keep* up. Since the 1960s, American technologists have been speculating about the possibility of an intelligence explosion brought on by the invention and distribution of super-intelligent computers. The thinking goes that after this hypothetical moment, often called the technological singularity, humans will be outpaced, outnumbered, or even ruled by machines. Films such as *I, Robot*; *The Matrix*; or the *Terminator* series are science-fiction predictions of this moment. For many theorists, a key moment will be the development of computers that can pass the Turing test.

The Turing test, popularized in the award-winning 2014 film *The Imitation Game*, is a test named after its creator, the brilliant Alan Turing (1950), and a thought experiment he invented in his seminal paper, "Computing Machinery and Intelligence." The Turing test is a relatively simple exercise designed to determine whether or not a theoretical machine has intelligence indistinguishable from that of a human.

What many people overlook, however, is an earlier paper by Turing (1937) called, "On Computable Numbers, with an Application to the Entscheidungsproblem." Although the paper is esoteric – it's written for professional logicians – the implications of this paper are arguably more significant than his discussion of the popularized Turing halting problem.

I'll skip over the math – a subject worthy of its own book – to summarize the significance of Turing's work to the creation of Bravespace workplaces. Turing's paper proves that there is no possible algorithm that could determine the solvability of a given problem – there is no algorithm that can say whether a given problem has or doesn't have a solution. In order to prove this, Turing invented a "machine" whose functioning forms the theoretical basis for today's computer processors, and then proves that this machine cannot answer specific questions.[1] Interestingly, a consequence of Turing's paper is that humans *can* determine

---

1. Specifically, Turing uses first-order logic to prove that Alonzo Church's lambda-calculus – a system of logic on which any natural function can be computed – was equivalent to his Turing machine. He then uses his Turing machine to prove that there can be no general process for determining whether a given formula written in lambda-calculus is provable. Like I said, this is thick stuff. If you're interested, I recommend Charles Petzold's *The Annotated Turing*.

"

Today's computers, super-computers, and quantum computers all must follow the rules of logic that underlie Turing's proof: there are and always will be some things that humans can do that machines cannot.

whether or not a given equation has a solution, even if it's difficult to find. In other words, Turing simultaneously invented and proved the limits of computational thinking. Today's computers, super-computers, and quantum computers all must follow the rules of logic that underlie Turing's proof: *there are and always will be some things that humans can do that machines cannot.* Yet despite this proof, and perhaps because of its inaccessibility, much popular media focuses on the threat posed by the abundance of machines in today's work places.

Fear of this threat is justified, since workers have been and continue to be replaced by machines that can perform their labor more efficiently and for longer periods of time, without fatigue, and can compute vast amounts of data much more quickly. The McKinsey Global Institute (2018) predicts that as early as 2030 robots and AI will force up to one-third of the American workforce to switch to new occupations.

As Turing proved, and as we all emphatically hope, there are some jobs that humans will always do. Which leaves us not so much with the question of the fate of humanity as machines take over, but rather the problem of how to organize and work with machines to find the right and best role for everyone, human or machine. As Kevin Drum (2017) said in *Mother Jones*, "Until we figure out how to fairly distribute the fruits of robot labor, [we are facing] an era of mass joblessness and mass poverty."

What is it that humans can do that robots can't? And how do we make sure that our job economy uses each of these resources to the fullest? Leaders should be asking three key questions today that will shape tomorrow's workplace regarding the trends of technology: What work is unique to humans? What role does work play in the health of society? How can machines reinforce what humans do best?

Work That's Unique to Humans

Turing proved that no machine can decide the solvability of a given math problem, but a person can. But that doesn't mean that we should all become mathematicians, seeking to determine solvability. Most experts agree that there is one area of human cognition that machines may never emulate – human connection. Getting the mix of pheromones, hormones, body language, intuition, emotions, and

“

We bring our need and our
talent for connection with other
human beings into every aspect
of our lives, including work.

so on just right in a machine will be extremely difficult, and has so far proved impossible. Imagine, for a moment, a machine comforting you in the doctor's office after a devastating diagnosis, a time when you most need someone to simply empathize with the shock and pain you feel. Or a robot motivating and inspiring a group of programmers to stay up all night to reach a deadline, when every fiber of their being thinks that it's crazy. These and countless other scenarios require nuanced, unique human contemplation, reflection, communication, and impact that is likely impossible for a machine of any type to replicate.

What's more, as Brené Brown (2012) says in her bestselling book *Daring Greatly*, "human beings are hard-wired for connection," and our need for loving, emotional, wholehearted contact with other human beings is as important to us as food, water, air, and shelter; in fact, we do connection very well. We bring our need and our talent for connection with other human beings into every aspect of our lives, including work. This need drives much about how we live together in communities, both at work and at home.

As AI and robots proliferate, a key echelon of work will endure. All the jobs requiring empathy, care, compassion, and connection, such as teaching, childcare, social work, nursing, counseling, primary care, leadership, and even customer service, will be relevant in a robotic future. At present, many of these jobs are found at the bottom of the wage and desirability pile, but in a machine-fueled future we might see increased demand and compensation for positions requiring intimate human connection.

All organizations should know which of their roles fall in the realm of "uniquely human" and consider how they will recruit, develop, and reward people to grow their skill and fluency in these jobs. People are not machines, which is a good thing for any job requiring human connection, inspiration, collaboration, leadership, trust, creativity, and intuition.

The Role Work Plays in the Overall Health of Society

What businesses do and how they do it impacts spheres of our lives well beyond the walls of a conference room. It is critical that we not limit our thinking about the role of working machines to that of merely the replacement of jobs. As jobs change, we see reverberant changes in the entire social construct of "work" – a construct relevant to the total health of our families, our neighborhoods, our cities, our nation, and our world. Figuring out how our two general categories of workers – machines and humans – are structured in our economies will determine whether each category is beneficial or detrimental to our society at large.

First, workers make money. Money buys food, shelter, and other commodities. The activity of buying things fuels economic growth – Economics 101. But if a robot takes my job, the whole system crumbles. I have no money to spend. As a result, the people around me stop getting paid, and so on. A simple change – the massive redistribution of the demand for employment – changes the global structure of economics.

It's critical that leaders think deeply about which currencies they exchange with their employees. What do you offer as an employer that matters to your workers? The complex bundle of cash, benefits, paid time off, meaning, a place to go, relationships, the ability to grow, etc. must be considered in order to elevate and reward people at work tomorrow.

We work for money so that we can buy food, shelter, and candy, yes. But, and this is my second point, we also work because it makes us matter. From ancient Greek philosopher Aristotle's *Nicomachean Ethics*, which states that work makes life meaningful, to Barry Schwartz's book, *Why We Work*, we're told that when we contribute to something or someone outside of ourselves, our purpose motivates us to keep going.

If people can't work, what happens to our drive for community? Or our eagerness to continue? As portrayed in

"

If people can't work, what happens to our drive for community? Or our eagerness to continue?

Pixar's computer-animated science fiction hit *WALL-E*, our life force likely atrophies and dies, leaving in its wake social problems including addiction, crime, family failures, depression, and the failure of social networks. We saw and felt this painful reality recently in the disenfranchisement of workers in the central United States and the United Kingdom, where those who were marginalized by the offshoring of manufacturing jobs and the perception of an elite that has lost touch with the needs of the people, influenced with disproportionate power the election of President Trump and Britain's exit from the European Union (Friedman 2016).

If machines eliminate jobs, and jobs give our lives meaning, what are we going to do to keep ourselves believing that we matter? The answers to this question are myriad and complex, but, fundamentally, the implications are that whether machines do our jobs tomorrow or not, we need somewhere to go and something to do. Work in the form of the jobs we hold benefits us individually and as a society in ways that are not only economic but also essential to our humanity.

How Machines Can Reinforce
What Humans Do Best

It's easy to feel threatened by the advent of automation, artificial intelligence, and machines that can do much of what we do better and faster. It's intimidating. In fact, when I watched the 2016 movie *Hidden Figures*, I was amazed that human beings once did work that is largely done today by computers: calculate huge and complex formulas quickly. As wonderful as the advent of computing was for NASA, all those good minds were out of work once the computers were up to speed. So how can machines support what we do best, not threaten it?

By speeding up data calculations, computers increase efficiency and the quality of results, which means that people have more time to think about the implications of whatever results are created. What does this mean? What should we do with this knowledge? The process of considering data and making it meaningful by taking action is uniquely human, and computing helps us do it more often.

The advent of big data means that we know more, by aggregating and comparing data, than ever before. Having a computer gather, store, and compare vast amounts of available information enables sweeping change. Beyond aggregating and comparing consumer data such as which toothpaste sells more, peppermint or spearmint, analyzing data helps us, as a worldwide community, to see such things as the implications of declining immunization rates

"

If machines eliminate jobs, and jobs give our lives meaning, what are we going to do to keep ourselves believing that we matter?

on community health or the long-term effect of an extend-ed commute time on productivity.

A second way that technology aids the work of people is by removing the rote and mind-numbing tasks that people hate anyway. Years ago, my sister worked on a speaker man-ufacturing line. Her job was to put a blue wire and a green wire on the back of a box. She did this 800 times a day, and her boss wanted her to do it 1,000. As Jamie said, "Yikes, it was mind-numbing work that didn't invite any of my intel-ligence or creativity. Moving from 800 to 1,000 really didn't feed my soul." Let's leave that work up to machines!

Third, machines and automation allow us to connect more with other people across common platforms. When medical records, for example, can be shared across agen-cies, physicians' decision-making, and thus healthcare, are improved because access to information is instant. Simi-larly, technology enables collaboration across time zones and geography since people everywhere can see the same

"

In Bravespace workplaces
of tomorrow people won't
simply be replaced with
machines; instead robots,
AI, and technology will be
leveraged to activate the best
possible decision-making and
partnerships of the people
who work in them.

data at the same time, can contribute, and can build on each other's ideas. These technological advances facilitate innovation, education, and collaboration in a wide variety of settings.

A fourth impact on how we work with technology is the advent of blockchain to democratize information, remove profiteers, and ensure data integrity. Decentralizing technology and wrapping information in shared repositories force us to use the consensus of many to drive decisions rather than the whims of one or a few. While this technology is not yet mainstream, it has the potential to bring out the best we can offer as human beings to make decisions that consider the common good.

AI and machine learning appear to be catapulting us into a future that's vastly different from the way we work today. The possibility of a cataclysmic, Terminator-esque future is just that, one possibility among many. Fortunately, the workers and leaders of today can shape the future of our workplaces.

There's no doubt that we'll work with technology in the future. But what are the implications of that technology on how we work and how we live? What we need right now are leaders who have the courage to ask, over and over, the essential questions that shape our workplaces. In Bravespace workplaces of tomorrow people won't simply be replaced with machines; instead robots, AI, and technology will be leveraged to activate the best possible decision-making and partnerships of the people who work in them.

In Chapter 3, I'll explore more deeply what it means to be a Bravespace workplace in the context of the inevitable continued rise of technology as our ever-present tool and partner, and profit as our ever-present motivator.

Chapter 3

ॐ

On Profit, Size, and Sharing Wealth

There is no greatness where there is no simplicity,
goodness and truth.

— Leo Tolstoy

WHEN I SHIFTED MY CAREER from non-profit management to the world of business, I did so in part to improve my own family's economics. As the primary earner in a dual-income family with two, then three, children, I needed to make more money. Business was a good way to do that, because the pay was higher and there was more room to grow in responsibility, but I felt conflicted about leaving behind my non-profit roots. I wondered if, in supporting my family, I had started to contribute to a flawed economic system that potentially damaged others' families. What might I, and others, have to give up in order to contribute to a successful society overall?

Profit Is Not Enough, But There May Be Cause for Hope

As grateful as I am for the benefits I've received working in business, I am at the same time astounded at the impact that the (often singular) focus on profit has on leaders, on the decisions they make, on the people who work for them, on the natural world we share, and on the communities in which businesses operate. Profit cannot continue to be the singular gold standard for companies of tomorrow. Not only are year-over-year profits unsustainable, but profit is losing status as a motivator for workers. Unlike previous generations of workers, Millennials and the generations behind them (Generation Z) care deeply about the "why" of the organization where they work. They hunger to be able to connect the dots between the work they do and the reason their company exists, both locally and globally. Proactive leaders of tomorrow's companies will spend time discussing and sharing the context of everything they do.

Kate Raworth (2017), radical economist and author of *Doughnut Economics*, says, "[The] fixation [on GDP as a nation's primary measure of progress] has been used to justify extreme inequalities of income and wealth coupled with unprecedented destruction of the living world. For the twenty-first century a far bigger goal is needed: meeting the human rights of every person within the means of our life-giving planet." It's time for every organization,

REFORM THE SYSTEMS

A successful society is a progress machine, turning innovations and fortuitous developments into shared advancement. America's machine is broken. Innovations fly at us, but progress eludes us. A thousand world-changing initiatives won't change that. Instead, we must reform the basic systems that allow people to live decently – the systems that decide what kind of school children attend, whether politicians listen to donors or citizens, whether people can tend to their ailments, whether they are paid enough, and with sufficient reliability, to make plans and raise kids.

There are a significant number of winners who recognize their role in propping up a bad system. They might be convinced that solving problems for all, at the root, will mean higher taxes, smaller profits, and fewer homes. Changing the world asks more than giving back. It also takes giving something up.

— Anand Giridharadas, *Winners Take All*

whatever its size and scope, to profoundly and deeply examine the reason it exists, and to practice, over and over again, telling that story to every stakeholder in its ecosystem. Doing so will provide the essential currencies for organizations to identify the human talent they require, even as they also leverage technology and automation.

"

It's time for every organization,
whatever its size and scope,
to profoundly and deeply
examine the reason it exists,
and to practice, over and over
again, telling that story to every
stakeholder in its ecosystem.

There is hope that things are changing for big companies. In its report, *The Rise of the Social Enterprise* (Agarwal et al. 2018), Deloitte argues that there's a tipping point of change for organizations today. Traditional organizations will become social enterprises (which combine revenue growth and profitmaking with respect and support of their environments and stakeholder networks). They name the three influencers of this sea change:

- The power of the individual is growing, with Millennials at the forefront.

- Businesses are expected to fill a widening leadership vacuum in society.

- Technological change is having unforeseen impacts on society even as it creates massive opportunities to achieve sustainable, inclusive growth.

These trends indicate what tomorrow's leaders must think about in order to thrive.

If You Win, I Lose Economics

The very economic system that I've grown up believing in has gone horribly awry, and the time has come for business to take a stronger role in fixing it. Oxfam's report citing the fact that the wealthiest 1 percent of people in the world hold almost 50 percent of the world's wealth, and that they're getting richer, is both old news and, at the same time, appalling (Hardoon 2015). American ethical and economic assumptions have inculcated in me a strong sense of surety that hard work pays off. I've always felt that earning a living for myself (from selling my garden squash by the roadside as a kid, to running a thriving consulting firm) would facilitate a lifestyle that worked for me (safety, shelter, healthcare, education for my children, comfort, small luxuries). And as a well-educated, white, middle-aged, able-bodied, heterosexual woman living in 21st-century America, I've benefited both from great privilege and from genuine effort. Along the way, though, the gap between my income and others' has widened in ways that degrade the quality of life for many. It's easy for me to keep making more money for myself and more profit for my clients' companies, but to do so requires turning a blind eye to what's happening to the fabric of global society. I cannot, in good conscience, do so. Can you? There's a better way, I believe, that demands of us a direct exploration of our contribution to the common good.

"

The very economic system that I've grown up believing in has gone horribly awry, and the time has come for business to take a stronger role in fixing it.

According to Oxfam's 2015 report, the world's richest 1 percent were expected to have as much wealth as the remaining 99 percent of the world by 2016. To put that another way, the report states that the 80 richest people on the planet will have the same wealth as the poorest 3.5 billion people:

80 people's wealth = 3.5 billion people's wealth

Oxfam's latest research is even more shocking (Pimentel 2018): "Last year (2017) saw the biggest increase in billionaires in history, one more every two days. This huge increase could have ended global extreme poverty seven times over. 82% of all wealth created in the last year went to the top 1%, and nothing went to the bottom 50%."

Experts speculate that politics and policies that favor big business and the wealthy have exponentially increased disparity between the über wealthy and the world's poorest. And the mega-tech companies are making things even worse. Nicholas Bloom (2017) wrote in

Harvard Business Review that "the result of countless strategic decisions in pursuit of [monetary] goals by Google and other elite companies throughout the world – not just in tech – has been to raise the compensation of some workers far more than others." Jamie Bartlett (2017) elaborated in the *Spectator*, arguing that "the meeting of techno-utopianism and profit-making is an unstoppable force, and it has a dark side. One result is that it is creating two almost entirely separate worlds." One world is getting richer, richer, and richer. One is getting poorer, poorer, and poorer – even though both groups work hard. With this wealth disparity come all the problems of people not thriving: poverty, violence, poor health, inequity, and more.

I wonder if we have deluded ourselves into thinking that, somehow, this is acceptable? That it is perfectly okay that our system creates more and more luxury and excess for a tiny few, while the vast majority live with less? Do we really believe that these inequalities are created by purely the hard work of the ultra-rich and, by default, tell ourselves a story

"

With this wealth disparity comes all the problems of people not thriving: poverty, violence, poor health, inequity, and more.

that the non-rich are simply not working hard enough? In the companies and organizations I work with, everyone is usually working hard, including those in the lower-wage jobs, such as night-shift or unskilled workers. Disproportionate pay to CEOs and shareholders from the wages of employees contributes to these inequities and erodes the meaning of hard work.

Without digging into the complexities of tax law and the policies that have created this situation, let's underline what Winnie Byanyima, Executive Director of Oxfam, said in their report: "It is time our leaders took on the powerful vested interests that stand in the way of a fairer and more prosperous world."

I remember that when I was a kid at school, some days I was short on lunch, and I borrowed from my friends to fill up. And some days my lunch box was full, and I shared with them. Metaphorically, it feels wrong that I eat a luscious, protein-rich meal while my classmate next to me gets by on stale Cheetos and fake juice. Businesses, whether micro-entities or megaliths that are "too big to fail," must evaluate how they reward excellence, and how they share for the common good.

Bravespace workplaces – organizations that know how to share for the common good – will lead in the work world of tomorrow. Some actions you could take if you seek to make your company fit for human life (a Bravespace workplace) in the context of wealth disparity, are:

"

Businesses, whether micro-entities
or megaliths that are "too big
to fail," must evaluate how they
reward excellence, and how they
share for the common good.

- Evaluate and understand your pay practices so that
  you can ensure equity across roles.

- Look at the pay gap between your lowest-paid
  employee and your CEO, and ask yourself if this ratio
  is appropriate.

- Make courageous change when inequity is found –
  do the right thing.

- Remember that all jobs in a company make it click –
  pay your leaders commensurate with their roles, and
  pay the employees who do your dirtiest jobs what
  they deserve.

- Look for ways to prevent waste inside your company
  so that there's more funding available for employee
  compensation, retirement, and benefits.

- Decide how much is enough (there is "enough") for
  you and your shareholders to make and proactively
  manage the overage responsibly by reinvesting

locally, sharing with employees, reducing prices, and making charitable gifts.

- Notice the gap between your wealthiest employees or shareholders and your poorest, and seek strategies with your leaders to reduce the gap.

- Keep your profit local.

- Pay the taxes you and your companies owe – these provide necessary social, law enforcement, judicial, and other services that make our society work for all.

My stomach turns at this wealth disparity. I'm disgusted. I'm proud of my success and have nothing to feel ashamed of (and neither do you). And while ultimately lawyers and policy makers set the policies that help to make the rich get richer, each of us can and must do more to end the disparity.

Winston Churchill said, "Where there is great power there is great responsibility." Changing the heartbreaking wealth disparity starts with responsible and accountable business owners and shareholders who are making a profit today and who have power. It's our job to notice the wealth disparity, to call out its inequity, and to actively and courageously make room for our fellow citizens of the world who also work hard, but don't have equal privilege and access. For our world economy to work, we cannot just turn our heads away from the "other 3.5 billion."

The growth of the global economy reached 3 percent in 2018, but as the United Nations (Drysdale 2018) says in

"

It's our job to notice the wealth disparity, to call out its iniquity, and to actively and courageously make room for our fellow citizens of the world who also work hard, but don't have equal privilege and access.

its most recent report, "Recent improvements in growth remain unevenly distributed across countries and regions. Economic prospects for many commodity exporters remain particularly challenging. Negligible growth in per capita GDP is anticipated in several parts of Africa, Western Asia, and Latin America and the Caribbean. The impacted regions combined are home to 275 million people living in extreme poverty. Without sustained economic growth, the chances of bringing that number to zero remain slim. To achieve the goals of eradicating poverty and creating decent jobs for all, it is essential to address the longer term structural issues that hold back a faster progress towards sustainable development."

Business that expands and benefits some but diminishes and harms others is ultimately good for no one. As noted writer and teacher Meg Wheatley (2002) says, "In a

"

Business that expands and benefits some but contracts and harms others is ultimately good for no one.

complex system, there is no such thing as simple cause and effect. There's no one person to blame, or to take the credit."

It's time for organizations to get back to basics and remember what the people who work for them need, and what the world needs.

The Common Good

Bravespace workplaces can and will be used to remedy the ills caused by unhealthy workplaces, wealth disparity, and the dark side of profit as a singular goal. The solutions aren't complex, but they aren't easy, either. The work requires action from every single employee, and from leaders especially. I've seen it happen in businesses all over the world, and it's a powerful experience to watch organizations get it right. What it takes is a recognition, acknowledgment, and mindset that we're connected, both locally and globally. When we do something here, it has an effect there, within organizations, between organizations, and in communities. We are interdependent, and organizations that understand this and operationalize it will become Brave-space workplaces, fit for human life.

My motivation for writing *Bravespace Workplace* comes from my frustration in knowing that we've understood for a long time what work conditions bring out the best in people, yet few companies have built themselves accordingly. I received my graduate degree in the study of people in systems (organizational development) in 1989. And while the theory and practice have incrementally advanced in the last nearly 30 years, we knew to a great extent then what we know now: human beings are what make organizations great, and when people feel connected, seen, and worthy at work, they perform better. Why can't we get it right after all this time? And why, despite what we know, is the state of work worsening?

The stories of recent workplace failures are big and dramatic. The #MeToo stories. The fall of Wall Street. Amazon's toxic workplace. Tech's bullying. Nike's gender and wage inequities. The digital age means that we can see more into the inner workings of organizations than we could before,

"

It's time for organizations to get back to basics and remember what the people who work for them need, and what the world needs.

> **"**
>
> We are interdependent, and
> organizations that understand this
> and operationalize it will become
> Bravespace workplaces, fit for
> human life.

and when we look inside many big companies, we feel dirty. How is it that we know what a sick organization looks like, and yet we can't seem to build many people-centered ones? Stanford University professor Jeffrey Pfeffer (2018) argues in his book, *Dying for a Paycheck*, that human sustainability should be as important as environmental stewardship. Pfeffer considers workplaces their own environmental hazard, citing data that suggest that unhealthy workplaces are responsible for approximately 125,000 deaths and $130 billion in excess costs in the United States each year. Clearly people at work aren't doing well.

The last 10-plus years of media attention focused on the workplace has made it seem that healthy workplaces are all about the perks: on-site dry cleaning, nap pods, and 24-hour coffee stations. Wild and crazy perks, largely coming out of Silicon Valley's explosive growth in the tech sector, include arcades, jobs without titles, and unlimited vacation time, which draw our attention to the surface aspects of a company. But what I've seen repeatedly is that what really matters to people are the subtle, internal perks. It seems that the media has been focusing on the wrong things. And the costs of this are grave.

Workplaces that aren't fit for human life accrue staggering costs. Gallup (2013) estimates that actively disengaged employees cost the United States $450 to $550 billion in lost productivity per year. A bad hire costs a company revenue, customers, and productivity, in addition to the hard costs of recruiting, training, and developing a new employee (as much as $50,000 in the United States), and the costs increase the longer a misfit employee is on the job.

Companies aren't the only ones paying for disengagement. The costs to individuals are shocking and terrifying. Jeffrey Pfeffer (2018) contends that many modern management commonalities such as long work hours, work-family conflict, and economic insecurity are toxic to employees, destroying engagement, increasing turnover, and destroying people's physical and emotional health. They are also inimical to company performance. The solution to this

"

Workplaces that aren't fit for human life accrue staggering costs.

horror isn't a workplace wellness program, which Pfeffer sees as a fairly worthless bandage applied to a self-inflicted wound.

Small Companies Provide A Glimmer of Hope

A small but critical caveat: there is some evidence that employees at small companies are doing better. According to Gallup research (2017a), the largest U.S. companies have the lowest levels of engagement, while businesses with fewer than 25 employees have the highest. And in one recent report, 75 percent of small business workers surveyed said they were "very" or "extremely" satisfied in their role with a small employer. There are a host of reasons for this, ranging from more flexible work arrangements, employees being able to see the impact they have, and non-cash incentives.

There's something important to learn from this research, and over the last 20 years I've noticed it in my consulting practice as well: The ability that leaders have to directly influence things within their control is much greater in small companies. The work that my colleagues and I have done with these smaller companies enabled their leaders to facilitate change more swiftly and with greater impact.

In Part II, I'll talk about workplaces themselves: What makes a workplace toxic? What makes it great?

PART II

࿇

Most Workplaces are
Unfit for Human Life

Chapter 4

❧

Toxic is Bad!

You can love a monster, it can even love you back, but that doesn't change its nature.

— Eliza Crewe, *Crushed*

A FELLOW WORKPLACE CONSULTANT AND I were talking about how surprised we were that every industry and every company had employees who were miserable, no matter what the sector. Whether an organization is large or small, public or private, or whether the employees are white collar or blue collar, there's always a possibility that the conditions at work will be bad for some employees. This chapter builds on our definition of what really counts in making a great workplace by expanding on the specific costs and impacts of toxicity at work.

I never cease to be amazed at the conditions in which we human beings can work. From ship-breaking in the port town of Alang, India, to assembly-line work or coal mining in the United States, some jobs are truly deplorable and toxic. But work is unavoidable for most of us, so we human beings do what we must.

For many of you reading *Bravespace Workplace*, the odds are that although some of the jobs in your company might be dirty or difficult, they're likely more desirable than the worst jobs out there. But toxic work doesn't have to be deadly to cause harm. The #MeToo movement in 2018 blew the lid off sexual predation, harassment, and intimidation and the devastating role they play for many in their jobs. In particular, the downfalls of powerful men in the media production world revealed threatening, manipulative, and sometimes illegal behavior that has caused us all to wonder, *Why haven't women been speaking up?*

What we're learning is that over the past 50 years people *have* spoken up about terrible behavior at work, but they've been ignored and harmed further. And although whistleblower laws are designed to protect people, speaking truth to power is dangerous to the whistle blowers in both small and catastrophic ways. Additionally, thousands of men and women in workplaces around the country have spoken

"

I never cease to be amazed at the conditions in which we human beings can work.

“

From long-overdue pay raises to
tyrant leaders who aren't held
accountable for bad behavior,
organizations frequently protect
and defend their status quo, even
when over time it makes them
inhospitable for humans.

about their #MeToo moments and the pain they caused,
even as they said to themselves, "I didn't think it was that
bad, compared to . . . ." We have adjusted our expectations of
work in ways that result in us not noticing what's bad for us.
It's not uncommon for me to start working with a company
and, during assessment, discover that the issues at hand
have been going on for a long time. From long-overdue pay
raises to tyrant leaders who aren't held accountable for bad
behavior, organizations frequently protect and defend their
status quo, even when over time it makes them inhospitable
for humans.

Most of us know the frog in boiling water parable, where
the frog placed in scalding water immediately fights to
jump out because of the pain. But the frog placed in cool
water that heats up slowly gets scalded as it incrementally

adjusts to the conditions over time. At work, we're a bit like frogs.

Workplaces face an onslaught of factors that threaten their ability to activate, enliven, and tenderly support the complex humans that we are. Here are the top five factors that I see play out in organizations repeatedly:

- **24/7 Access and Our Devices.** We're addicted to our devices. We carry them on our bodies and access them every few minutes. This means that our work is always ready to find us, to activate us, and to urge us to respond. A lot about this is good: it enables us to work anywhere, anytime. It speeds things up, so we can solve problems faster. It connects us globally. But the toxicity creeps in to violate and sabotage us. We need work to meet our basic needs, and our devices convince us that if we aren't always on, we're not good enough and we'll be regarded as not working as much as others. Speeding up response and thinking time also sometimes simultaneously erodes

"

We work to contribute, to be seen, and to connect, and our devices seduce us into thinking that we should be connected all the time.

❝

The speed of our connection moves us fleetingly from one thing to another, with very little time to think and to add value by learning and growing.

the quality of our decisions and our collaborative abilities. We work to contribute, to be seen, and to connect, and our devices seduce us into thinking that we should be connected all the time.

Digital media, email, text, and even collaboration hubs such as Slack are accessed by our devices, and they offer us things that are markedly different from our essential human need for connection. They're not necessarily bad – in fact, these applications often help us to be productive and connected – but the speed of our connection moves us fleetingly from one thing to another, with very little time to think and to add value by learning and growing. We need to feel supported at work, yet our fragmented interactions with one another on these devices result in us often feeling more alone than ever. And we need to be able to make our lives work, but our devices have inserted themselves into every facet of our personal lives as well, showing up at our workouts, our dinner tables, our bedtimes with our kids, and even our bedrooms.

In addition, the media and advertising tell us that perfection is the ideal, which makes us feel that we're never good enough. And our devices make us feel even worse. We compare ourselves to our bosses' seeming heroism at working all hours and find ourselves wanting. We see other people's curated social media life, and we feel small because something is missing in our lives. We become numb and isolated, and the cycle continues.

Bravespace workplaces of the future help to define the role that our devices have in our lives and the extent to which work intrudes on our personal lives. A Bravespace workplace is where we can show up as we are, both worthy and flawed, and do great things together, as human beings, with our strengths and weaknesses shaping how we partner and how we attack difficult tasks. As tools for productivity, our devices can be helpful, but when the devices themselves eat away our time and our confidence, we need to find an alternative. The rise of screen addiction among our children is a symptom of this toxic element of our workplaces that deadens our humanity: they learn from and copy us.

- **Lack of Inclusion.** The demographics of our work worlds are changing fast. The workforce is aging and

"

Most people consider it a competitive advantage to have diverse minds working to solve problems; in other words, diversity is a good thing.

will continue to do so; it's also becoming more diverse and, overall, more educated. Most people consider it a competitive advantage to have diverse minds working to solve problems; in other words, diversity is a good thing. Despite this, inclusion still stymies us at work. Women, people of color, LGBTQQ+, people with disabilities, and other outsider groups continue to lag behind white men in their wages, power, and authority in almost every sector, despite the increase in their representation in the workplace. In addition, the state of white men as a group is precarious. They exhibit high rates of suicide, addiction, and alienation, in addition to being the majority of perpetrators of mass gun violence. We need a new way to talk about inclusion in a way that leads to practicing inclusion, a way that honors and benefits everyone. White men, who are typically outside of diversity and inclusion conversations, must be

"

Bravespace workplaces are ones in which race, gender, sexual orientation, and all the other things that make us both different and the same are discussed.

invited in, to learn, contribute, and benefit from the exploration of how limiting systemic advantages to one group has created inequities at work that we can (and must) change.

Bravespace workplaces are ones in which race, gender, sexual orientation, and all the other things that make us both different and the same are discussed. Leaders of these workplaces eschew political correctness by tackling the truly hard issues that continue to stratify our society at home and at work.

- **Erosion of Time to Think.** Sean was a client who walked through my door seeking help. Promoted several times because of his hard work and keen mind, he was promoted again to manage a larger team. After six months on the job he was flailing and losing the respect of his staff. Leaders often get promoted without understanding what work they'll have to let go of in order to assume their new role, or without support from others in gaining that understanding. Instead of empowering and teaching his employees to use their creativity, discretion, and judgment to solve problems so that he wouldn't have to anymore, Sean was "heroically" doing it all. As a result, he lacked any time in his meeting-filled days to bring forward that which was most precious to his employer.

Chris Carmichael, trainer of cycling phenom Lance Armstrong, revolutionized endurance training by incorporating rest into the rotation. Athletes can't go full tilt day after day and get better and better – their bodies need time to rebuild and recover. That applies to all of us. Our brains at work also need time to rest, recover, and think. Modern workplaces with their frenetic pace leave little time for simply thinking. This means that we don't do our best work. Time to think doesn't have to mean a month at an ashram in India. It can be a blank hour in the calendar, a walking reflection, or a conversation about ideas before action. Bravespace workplaces enable us to resist the urge to overdo. Time is overtly

〝

Bravespace workplaces enable us
to resist the urge to overdo.

ide for the people who work there to consider
, to respond, to analyze, and to think. When
appens, the quality of ideas improves, people
contribute more, and optimum results increase.

- **Leaders Who are Bad for People.** I have seen
company after company ignore the dead weight of
terrible managers for a host of reasons. The most
common reason is that they are high producers, and
therefore in a protected class, untouchable. When
companies ignore bad managers, everyone suffers.
The people who work for these toxic leaders wonder
why no one is doing anything, they're demoralized,
and they're confused by the gap between the values
espoused by these leaders and the toxic world that
the employees live in every day. With no attention
from senior leaders, these situations usually get
worse and result in employee churn, low team
motivation and morale, and bad behaviors from team
members. When the leader behaves badly, it signals
that the behavior is okay and that no one minds. And
inappropriate and bad behavior invites more of the
same. There has been an uptick in bullying at work
and in school since President Trump was elected, and

"

When companies ignore bad
managers, everyone suffers.

"

Employees tune in, imprint, and copy what they see done by the leaders in their organization. In Bravespace workplaces leaders who are bad for people are swiftly and effectively dealt with.

that illustrates this dynamic: "If he can get away with it then I can too." "It violates all the norms and the niceties of how one should behave," said Gary Namie, director and cofounder of the Workplace Bullying Institute. "What it's exposing is the very, very dark side of our society."

Leaders in Bravespace workplaces who are people-centered (they believe that people are what make companies great) and have demonstrated the ability to connect well with employees and colleagues are purposely invested in. And when leaders don't act in accordance with the cultural values and norms professed by the organization, there are swift consequences. Employees tune into, imprint, and copy what they see done by the leaders in their organization. In Bravespace workplaces leaders who are bad for people are swiftly and effectively dealt with.

- **Failure to Tell the Truth.** When I work with companies of all types, a central piece of the work is the development of the norms and skills needed to have hard conversations. We often struggle mightily at work to tell our truth, to reveal what we feel, particularly when it comes to telling people of the impact they have on us, and to navigate conflicts. People at work have adopted behaviors that work around straight talk, including triangulation (telling our feelings to someone else, not the person we have an issue with), gossip (talking smack about someone behind their back), and avoidance (just not dealing with the situation), which is the most common behavior. This lack of truthfulness, and the masking of real feelings and needs, results in disconnection, isolation, and frustration at work. Decades of business ethics that kept emotions out of the workplace have resulted in those emotions leaking out unproductively, at inappropriate times, and in devastating ways, leading to stress-related illness and employee absenteeism.

The values and methods needed for handling conversations about difficult issues are commonplace in Bravespace workplaces. Leaders at every level are taught ways to be kind and clear while also delivering direct feedback. Emotions at work are viewed as essential for important (even if hard) conversations that lead to creativity and innovations.

Toxic workplaces can look healthy on the outside, with a beautiful annual report, a fitness center, and ergonomic chairs. But what makes an organization fit for human life is the opposite of the five trends we just examined. These organizations stay healthy by drawing boundaries around work time and not expecting 24/7 digital connection, creating cultures of inclusion, designing time to think, fostering leaders who are good for people, and expecting (and modeling) real and true (even when difficult) conversations.

"

Decades of business ethics
that kept emotions out of the
workplace have resulted in
those emotions leaking out
unproductively, at inappropriate
times, and in devastating ways,
leading to stress-related illness and
employee absenteeism.

Chapter 5

ॐ

Workplace = Bravespace
A New Definition

Brave doesn't always involve grand gestures.
Sometimes brave looks more like staying when you
want to leave, telling the truth when all you want to
do is change the subject.

— Shauna Niequist

THERE'S A DEEPENING ANXIETY that robots and technology will remove humans from the workplaces of tomorrow. But doing so would be a mistake, because the profound differentiator for most companies remains the people who work for them. It's people at work who bring empathy, connection, magic, warmth, understanding, joy, creativity, imagination, beauty, and innovation to organizations as they build things, serve customers, and meet their mission.

In order to crack the code on creating workplaces that are fit for human life, I propose a new way to describe healthy,

"

It's people at work
who bring empathy,
connection, magic,
warmth, understanding,
joy, creativity, imagination,
beauty, and innovation to
organizations as they build
things, serve customers,
and meet their mission.

People cannot be
defined in one paradigm
or put in one box.

or great, workplaces: *Bravespace.* In Bravespace workplaces the absolute best in the human beings who work there is cultivated, despite our imperfect and complicated human motivations, needs, and issues. In Bravespace workplaces, people can face the risks, emotional exposure, uncertainty, and vulnerability that come with work, knowing that their courage is supported and invited. The leaders of Bravespace workplaces know that people aren't machines, and they treat them accordingly. People are strong and fragile, smart and thoughtless, complex and basic, diverse and similar. We are complex and beautiful, and predicting what we'll do in different circumstances is almost impossible.

People cannot be defined in one paradigm or put in one box. Bravespace workplaces are people-centered because their leaders deeply understand that people make all the good things happen at work. In this chapter I'll explore the currencies that really matter to people today at work, as well as expand on the implications of a new definition of work for how we run organizations tomorrow.

Happiness Isn't Enough

Over the course of my career, I've heard leaders from all sectors, when interpreting my overarching messages to them, say "So, we need to do things that make people happy at work, right?" They think that happiness is a permanent state that we can create with a magic wand. Creating workplaces fit for human life, and paying conscious attention to

> ❝
>
> In Bravespace workplaces, people can face the risks, emotional exposure, uncertainty, and vulnerability that come with work, knowing that their courage is supported and invited.

the soft stuff of people-centered leadership and culture, is not simply about making people happy at work.

What after all, is "happy"? Happiness in Shakespearean times was equated to prosperity and good fortune. Going further back to ancient Greece (Aristotle 2011), "Happiness . . . signifie[d] more than mere sentiment or feeling, more than the pleasure of the moment or even of a series of satisfied desires. . . . [Happiness] encompassed the excellence specific to human beings as human beings. . . . The question of how to be happy [was] the question of how to live well as a human being."

Today the word *happiness*, as defined by *Merriam-Webster* (2018a), refers to a "state of well-being and contentment, or a pleasurable and satisfying experience." It's certainly not a bad thing for employees to experience their workplace as pleasurable, but let's face it: organizations exist for a host of other, larger purposes, which drive their behavior and their processes far more profoundly than merely ensuring employee happiness. This is as it should be. Organizations large and small are created to meet a specific purpose (their mission), making them separate and distinct from the aggregate of individuals who work for them. Employment starts with the needs of the organization, and the needs of the employees come second. If there is no work to organize around, there is no need for shared work. In other words, where there is no employer, there is no employee.

Going back to our premise, then, that people are what make companies great, it's incumbent on every organization to ensure that the people who work there thrive, which is different from mere happiness, which is both transient and fleeting. Workers thrive in Bravespace workplaces. Sure, on some days we hope to feel pleasure at work and satisfaction: happiness. But when a worker solves a tough

"

Creating workplaces fit for human life, and paying conscious attention to the soft stuff of people-centered leadership and culture, is not simply about making people happy at work.

＂

Real thriving at work, in any job, is about knowing that we're contributing to something bigger than ourselves.

problem, or spends a long and difficult day at work, they lay their head down on their pillow at night satisfied at their contribution, not because it made them happy, but because it mattered. Thriving at work invites many other human experiences beyond happiness: complexity, frustration, challenge, creativity, loss, confusion, inspiration, hope, failure. What if we reframe the subject to be less about making sure that employees are happy, and more about whether they feel alive, are thriving, and feel sure that what they're doing matters?

Real thriving at work, in any job, is about knowing that we're contributing to something bigger than ourselves. When we feel this, we're propelled to connect, to produce, to learn, to listen, and to contribute. It's the nuance of being human at work. We seek to feel seen, valued, and respected, and when we don't, we become disheartened, unmotivated, and numb.

When leaders of any organization focus on making people happy, they might as well just bring chocolate and beer to work; both of these cause short-term positive feelings, and temporary numbing. When leaders instead focus on facilitating ways in which every employee can thrive, they are required to dig deeper, beneath the surface, to reach what we as human beings need to function well. To help employees feel alive at work, leaders must look more closely and consider what motivates people, what makes their hearts sing, why they work, and what they dream.

Professors Andre Spicer and Carl Cederstrom (2015) address the nuance of oversimplifying worker motivations to simple happiness: "We think there is a strong case for rethinking our expectation that work should always make us happy. It can be exhausting, make us overreact, drain our personal life of meaning, increase our vulnerability, make us more gullible, selfish and lonely. Most striking is that consciously pursuing happiness can actually drain the sense of joy we usually get from the really good things we experience."

''

To help employees feel alive at work, leaders must look more closely and consider what motivates people, what makes their hearts sing, why they work, and what they dream.

"

Thriving at work invites many other human experiences beyond happiness: complexity, frustration, challenge, creativity, loss, confusion, inspiration, hope, failure. What if we reframe the subject to be less about making sure that employees are happy, and more about whether they feel alive, are thriving, and feel sure that what they're doing matters?

Days in a job are made joyous in part by the contrast with the dark and difficult ones. Let's stop talking about happiness and focus on helping each other feel alive at work – bringing our huffing, puffing, thinking, sweating, engaging, arguing, stubborn, and brilliant selves to work in a way that matters far more than mere happiness.

Work is Work, but the Times They are a-Changin'

When I was young, my parents asked me to do chores around the house. I would whine and moan about it, as most kids do, no matter how easy or hard the task. My Mom would say, "Well, they don't call it work for nothing!"

Our work is supposed to cause us to sweat and to strive; the word *work* describes an activity or effort toward a specific result. Academics and researchers have examined the complexities of what happens when people work together in organizations since the industrial revolution, which marked a giant migration from agrarian society to an industrialized one. It was then that people moved to urban areas and congregated in companies for mass production and the efficiency impossible in the quilted fabric of farms across the nation.

As early as the late 1800s, Max Weber (1958) wrote about his concern that the Industrial Revolution's focus on efficiency constrained employees to a kind of prison and "stripped a worker of their individuality." Organizational development, organizational behavior, and organizational psychology in the years since have advanced theories of what it takes to harness the best that people have to offer at work in order to benefit the company and, ultimately, society at large.

The intersection of what's good for people and what's good for business contains numerous paradoxes for leaders and employees to navigate. For example, the paradox between what's good for the individual and what's good for the group; the paradox between profitability and work/life balance; the paradox between worker safety and efficiency; the paradox between fair wages and owner income. Occupational stress, work's impact on families, ephemeral balance, employee wellness, productivity, and other elements of the impact of work on people remains fascinating, epitomized by the volume of articles, podcasts, books, and theories about how we work and what is best for us.

The modern workplace is in great flux. There are new productivity tools introduced each week that are supposed to help us get more work done faster. We're connected with colleagues worldwide via a multitude of devices that are always on. The gig economy produces more and more independent workers with flexibility and choice but without employee benefits or job security. Companies merge and sell. These changes in the world of work have both positive and negative effects on people globally. Since people make companies great, and because people contribute more when they are thriving at work, it's helpful to consider trends that impact the creation of workplaces fit for human life. Cammie Dunaway and I (Carrick and Dunaway 2017) outlined the following key trends in our book *Fit Matters*, and they remain relevant and timely today:

- **New and Ambiguous Roles.** New jobs appear every year that did not previously exist – Social Media Coordinator, Director of First Impressions, Growth Hacker, to name a few. In our technology-driven economy of service businesses, where information (data) rules, jobs are morphing in novel and unanticipated ways. Gone are the days when the selection of one career path in a known profession (doctor, lawyer, civil servant) was a sure thing for life. And even in known professions, paths are changing quickly; for example, physicians can review MRIs from thousands of miles away without seeing the patient, and marketers may work only in digital media realms. And this pace will increase – it's estimated that 65 percent of jobs that will be available when today's kindergartners graduate college don't exist today. (Rosen 2011)

- **Increase in the Desire for Meaning.** The days when a job was just to make money to provide for the family have passed; the purpose behind our desire to work has shifted. Increasingly, new workers (especially the Millennial generation) seek meaning when they look for a job. This means that despite the perks, promotions, pathways, or professions of a particular role, if employees can't find a higher purpose in their work or company, they'll feel disconnected, disenfranchised, and, ultimately, misfit. While it's possible that this has always been so, it feels more acute today when long-term employer-employee relationships are not a given. In fact, most people can expect to have 11 to 13 jobs during their lifetimes.

- **Flexibility as a Currency.** Workers today aren't satisfied with traditional nine-to-five work hours; they prefer to schedule their work around hobbies, caregiving, and lifestyle choices. This alters the traditional construct of an office, where people sit in cubicles or meeting rooms and crank out documents and information. People want portability and flexibility in the way they work.

- **Information Overload.** Today the availability of data isn't an issue: we're swimming in information every minute of the day, accessible by various devices and from locations as wide-ranging as a boat in the Arctic to our neighborhood Starbucks. Access to information isn't an issue; the issue is knowing what information to pay attention to, and whether that information is relevant to our decision-making process.

- **Distributed Companies and Teams.** Digital connection anywhere, anytime, means that people and work are no longer organized in traditional settings. People work across platforms, time zones, languages, and cultures more than ever before, putting increased demand on communication, clarity, and team cohesion. This trend puts pressure on employees at all levels to build social capital with people in all directions to get things done. It's not only feasible but also likely that you have a boss or teammates you never actually see in person because they live across an ocean.

- **Speed.** Things happen faster than ever in the world of work today, resulting in increasing stress and pressure for workers to assimilate huge volumes of data quickly. They make decisions fast for fear of falling behind or missing an opportunity. The internalized pressure to do more with less, in half the time, adds up to a head-down, shoulders-bunched, running-in-place iconoclastic image of American workers – all action, very little reflection.

- **Cloud Workers/Outsourcing.** An increasing number of workers are freelancers today, and companies are frequently reducing costs by outsourcing work to part-time or occasional workers to avoid overhead (Nunberg 2016). This combination provides flexibility, but it fails to deliver stability and predictability for workers, which impacts their ability to keep ahead of living expenses, plan for big life events, and take advantage of company benefits. This trend has implications for the social contract between employer and employee in terms of long-term security, which affects individuals, families, and communities.

- **Sustainability Imperative.** Business growth for growth's sake is being replaced with purposeful, responsible growth, in ways that minimize the impact on the environment, people, and natural resources. Greed is replaced by values, profit partners with impact, and business is increasingly leveraged as a force for good. The rise of social entrepreneurship means that more and more companies not only make money, they also make a difference. The new business status of benefit corporations, embraced by strong consumer brands such as Patagonia, Dansko, Method, and Ben & Jerry's, are evidence of the consumer's interest in products that, at a minimum, do no harm. This has implications for employees, particularly given their increasing desire to finding meaning and purpose at work.

- **Inclusion Imperative.** Numerous factors impact the extent to which organizations seek more diverse pools of workers. Having people with diverse experiences, views, and abilities makes companies more creative and innovative, if they can navigate conflict. Beyond quotas and government regulations regarding equal employment opportunity, organizations increasingly seek workers who represent their client populations. There are still challenges with recruitment and retention of minorities (aka outsiders,) but the tide has turned when it comes to an interest in and commitment to diversity and, even more importantly, inclusion.

- **Overwhelmed Workers.** Lightning-fast changes in global markets have created an overwhelmed workforce. The popularity of yoga, meditation, and mindfulness exercises shows that we hunger for relief from feeling overloaded, inundated, and overstretched with the vast quantities of information and work demands we face day after day. Brigid Schulte (2014) writes of both the costs of our work-hard culture to human beings as well as ways to reclaim our lives together.

- **Generational Turnover.** Baby boomers are entering retirement, and more than a third of the workforce (an estimated 56 million Americans) consisted of Millennials in 2017 (Cilluffo and Cohn 2017). The transfer of power, knowledge, experience, authority, and influence is well underway, and will undoubtedly continue to change how we work. Millennial workers are motivated by priorities that are different from those of previous generations, and they're changing how work unfolds.

- **New and Evolving Rules for Managing.** The command and control management approaches of old are no longer de rigueur. California's Silicon Valley firms and those from other hubs of innovation continue to establish paradigm-shifting ways to organize and motivate people at work, redefining what it means to manage and to lead. From completely flat structures where everyone is paid the same, to team-based approaches where no one is boss, to the question of what will work is wide open. This trend impacts the relationships between bosses and employees and between employees and each other.

New World of Work = New Definition

In the face of these shifting sands, how do we determine what people really need to perform well at work and to thrive as human beings?

We know what it takes to create circumstances at work that breed inspiration, performance, creativity, love, and

"

We know what it takes to create circumstances at work that breed inspiration, performance, creativity, love, and delight.

"

The list of what we can do at and through work is limitless when we get what we need from work.

delight. And yet we fail to do what it takes, time after time, leaving human beings at work disengaged, disenfranchised, angry, frustrated, and leaving the best they have to offer at home.

As I mentioned in Chapter 1, there are seven needs that work should fulfill: to meet our basic requirements, to contribute, to be seen, to connect, to learn, to feel supported, and to make our lives work. Workplaces that fulfill these needs are fit for human life. They are Bravespace workplaces. When these needs are fulfilled, we can do it all. We can use our bodies to engage in hard, manual labor. We can create beauty or design items that inspire and delight. We can talk to people and get them to do amazing things together. We can innovate. We can apply our knowledge, training, and skills to a task. We can build things. We can negotiate. We can sell. We can heal others. We can serve food. The list of what we can do at and through work is limitless when we get what we need from work.

In Chapter 6 I'll go into greater detail about these seven needs that work should fulfill, and I'll examine the critical questions that leaders at every level should consider in their quest to create a workplace fit for human life. Ensuing chapters will offer tools for learning how to actually create that workplace, and the inspiration to use those tools.

Chapter 6

Instructions for Human Beings

People need to be encouraged. People need to be reminded of how wonderful they are. People need to be believed in – told that they are brave and smart and capable of accomplishing all the dreams they dream and more. Remind each other of this.

— Stacey Jean Speer

WHEN MY CHILDREN WERE YOUNG, their Dad and I used to talk about how we wished they had come with instruction books, with descriptions of what we should do in certain situations:

- What exactly is the time limit for letting him cry himself to sleep when each second seems like a lifetime of pain?

- What's the best way to compliment her beauty without making it the most important thing to her?

"

"People problems" are the most-cited reason that organizations call me.

One key reason why employers must understand and strive to meet the needs of their employees at work: to ensure that they thrive there, bringing their best talents to work every day, which improves business results and organizational value.

- When they won't sleep, but you feel like you'll die if *you* don't sleep, what's the best approach for dealing with it?

But, alas, we're not born with a guide. We humans are complex in our motivations, our emotional reactions, our ways of thinking, our fears, and our stories. And when we get to be of working age, guess what? We bring all that complexity and diversity right smack dab into the workplace.

As we discussed earlier, there are seven needs we have that work should fulfill. In this chapter we'll explore these needs and construct a playbook for how employers can meet the needs of their employees at work. I'm not compelled to ask employers to meet employee needs only because it's the right thing to do, it feels good, or it makes people happy. My lived and professional experience points to one key reason why employers must understand and strive to meet the needs of their employees at work: to ensure that they thrive there, bringing their best talents to work every day, which improves business results and organizational value. After all, people make companies great.

"People problems" are the most-cited reason that organizations call me. Almost invariably, the problem is with a particular person or between some particular people. In our assessment phase we hear about the specific dynamics of Tom or Andrea or whoever is either causing or contributing

"

People are messy. We're complex and diverse and hard to understand without spending time together and communicating. We have needs, many of them, and we don't always know exactly what they are or how to meet them.

Most of us come to work wanting to do a good job.

to the problem. Many clients have said to me, "This would be easy if it weren't for the people." Ah, yes.

Someone who calls us is usually looking for a) hope – if they could have solved this on their own they surely would have – and b) a playbook – how can they change or influence a particular person in order to get a better outcome. People are messy. We're complex and diverse and hard to understand without spending time together and communicating. We have needs, many of them, and we don't always know exactly what they are or how to meet them.

Most of us come to work wanting to do a good job. It's part of our identity, and central to our sense of ourselves, to feel competent and worthy in our lives, and our lives include our work. In my experience with thousands of people in many workplaces over the years, I have not met one person who had a truly nefarious intention. We don't mean to cause problems at work, but we get all tangled up.

While writing *Fit Matters* with my co-author Cammie Dunaway, I was amazed that every time we talked to someone about work fit, they had a story to tell about jobs they'd loved or jobs they'd hated. The stories about the jobs they'd loved always sounded like stories about a fun family picnic. When we asked what they had loved about their job, they would say things such as:

- "I just feel that people care about me here."
- "It's fun to come to work every day!"
- "I can't imagine working with a boss I respect more!"

- "I've looked for this job my whole career."

These were the best conversations, although they were rare. In book research and in my consulting practice over the last 30-plus years, most stories I've heard are of misery:

- "I can't wait to get out of this job."
- "I'm looking for another job – this one sucks."
- "The time goes so slowly at work every day."
- "Does my boss think I'm an idiot?"

With *Fit Matters*, Cammie and I attempted to foster hope for people, that work didn't have to suck the life out of them. We offered tools and practical approaches for people seeking new jobs to help them find their ideal setting, and for people already in a job to craft their way to more positive experiences at work. We wanted to give employees the power to find fit, rather than leaving it up to chance.

Repeatedly since *Fit Matters* came out, feedback has been positive about the framework we offered for work fit. In conversations with people and in reviews of the book, we hear repeatedly that the six elements we introduced capture what people are looking for in a job. Here are the six elements that determine whether an employee is likely to thrive at work:

- **Meaning Fit** is great when you feel that what you do matters.

- **Job Fit** is great when the responsibilities of your job align with your talents and provide opportunities for growth.

- **Culture Fit** is great when your values and beliefs are compatible with the practices of your employer.

- **Relationship Fit** is great when you like and respect the people you work with and receive appropriate support and trust to do your job.

- **Lifestyle Fit** is great when your life outside of work is supported by your employer's policies and practices.

- **Financial Fit** is great when you feel that you're paid fairly and when what your employer offers (salary, bonus, benefits, perks, and allowances) meets your needs.

Our research pointed to the fact that work fit always requires a trade-off – there is no perfect fit – and it's temporally sensitive, meaning that our needs change over the course of our lives and what we need at one stage of our careers may not be what we need in another. By thinking about the six elements of work fit, we can evaluate the opportunities we seek, whether it's a new job or to modify our current work situation to strengthen the match between what we, as unique individuals, need at work and what our employer offers.

For employers, the considerations of the six elements of work fit are more complicated, since redesigning your organization to fit each individual employee's needs is difficult.

For employers, then, I recommend designing the organization from the stripped-down, more essential needs that human beings bring to the workplace: the seven needs that work should fulfill that I identified in Chapter 1. Ironically, designing a company to be fit for human life by consciously meeting the needs of the people who work there isn't always intuitive.

Can't We Just Do the Work?

I can't count the number of leaders whom I've had to convince that the work we would do together would have an impact on their company's bottom line. They listen to me with faces of incredulity, doubt, and skepticism. And yet, invariably, when they experience the work, whether it's in the realm of leadership, team, culture, or conflict, they feel the benefit, and we never have to repeat that conversation. Though they're hard to measure, the ephemeral elements of being a Bravespace workplace are tangibly felt.

For example, I once worked with a very charismatic leader. And his company got results. But when the wheels started to come off the bus of his company, he became

"

The ephemeral elements of being a Bravespace workplace are tangibly felt.

"

The only thing more expensive than an employee leaving is an employee who is miserable and stays.

petulant with me. "Moe, I hear that people are (insert descriptive negative state of being here), but this is, after all, a business. Right? It's not summer camp."

His company had more than double the average for employee turnover (21 percent.) And the exit interviews revealed deep problems. People said things such as, "I don't need to come to work every day afraid my manager is going to publicly humiliate me." "My husband is threatening to divorce me because I work every evening and weekend and we have little kids." I answered this CEO with words I have said many times, "You're right, it's 'just work.'" And then I asked him a question I knew he would get, "What will happen if you have to rehire 20 percent of your employees every year just to stay even?" Ka-ching! – money talks.

Any group is only as fast as its slowest member. Companies require people to do the jobs they need done. People need Bravespace workplaces in order to do their best work or they'll leave. Either actually or just mentally – the only thing more expensive than an employee leaving is an employee who is miserable and stays.

Work is not meant to be summer camp. But people need to thrive while working, and when they do, it's good for business. By *thrive* I mean, and *Merriam-Webster* (2018b) agrees, more than just survive or get by: to "grow vigorously, to prosper, to flourish." Most of us have, at some point in our lives, had that job that's just feeding us, a job where we were just marking time. But the jobs where we thrive can elevate any mundane work situation, and then we're in a Bravespace workplace.

When I traveled in Rwanda with a client, I was assigned a young driver and guide, Moses, whom I adored (we had many hours together during several trips.) His hours were long, his pay low. One hot, arduous travel day I asked him why he stayed with the job, given its difficulties. I remember his response so clearly: "I get to meet people from all over the world and help them see my country. I feel so lucky! I'm a good driver, and I think my boss knows that and cares about me."

It's not rocket science to understand what it takes to design and lead a workplace fit for human life, but it's not easy, either. People are diverse, needy, and complex. So what do employees really want from their employers? Recall from

"

Work is not meant to be summer camp.

"

It's not rocket science to understand what it takes to design and lead a workplace fit for human life, but it's not easy, either.

earlier chapters that there are seven needs people have that work should fulfill:

- To meet our basic requirements – to make enough money or non-cash compensation to provide food, clothing, shelter, and safety
- To contribute – to do something that matters to someone
- To be seen – and known
- To connect – in real ways, with other people
- To learn – and become better
- To feel supported – to be able to be brave knowing that there are risks
- To make our lives work – to be able to do the things that matter to us and are ours to do

Some of these needs, such as pay, are obvious, and employees negotiate for them. But most of people's other needs lurk within, neither named nor directly observable by their employers. People can't name what they need from work because these work needs are so basically connected to their essential needs as human beings that they don't differentiate them.

A study called the Grant Study is one of the longest running studies on human development. This study has run since 1938, and it has followed 268 men, who started as Harvard undergraduates, for 75 years. A study of this magnitude is valuable not only because of its length, but also for its range. Data was collected on practically everything – physical traits, family relationships, financial status, health, diet, habits, IQ, and much more. George Vaillant (2012) was the director of the study for more than 30 years, and he published a summary of his insights. He cited seven major factors that contribute to healthy aging and happiness. They are:

- Education
- Stable marriage
- Healthy weight
- Exercise
- Not smoking
- Not abusing alcohol
- Employing mature adaptations

He concluded that good social skills and coping methods are crucial to overall health and wellbeing, but the most telling aspect of the study came when the subjects' relationships and their life satisfaction were analyzed. There

"

"Happiness is love. Full stop."

were direct links between having a warm relationship with a mother on the one hand and financial success, mental health in old age, and career effectiveness (among others) on the other. A warm relationship with a father manifested itself in a decreased likelihood of adult anxiety and an increased ability to play, as well as a general feeling of happiness.

For all of us who feel that we're on an elusive quest for happiness, Valliant's final thought is remarkable. He finished by saying that the Grant Study points "to a straightforward, five-word conclusion: Happiness is love. Full stop."

Relationships Are the Key to Happiness at Work, as in Life

We cannot achieve happiness at work without warm relationships. Happiness is in the development of relationships and the moments we connect as people. So perhaps the most essential ingredient for what we need at work is fruitful, connected relationships. For any organization that has employees, a focus on healthy relationships at work is essential. You might be nodding your head right now, saying "duh." I know, it seems so easy. But in truth, we experience our company primarily through our immediate supervisor,

"

We cannot achieve happiness at work without warm relationships.

so our relationship with that person is critical to whether we thrive. No matter how accessible and connecting the CEO or owner are, if the person we directly work for alienates us, we experience work negatively.

Warm and healthy relationships at work require trust and self-awareness; both are big subjects that we'll tackle in Chapter 8: The Human Essentials. Until we get there, a good starting place for bringing out the best in the people who work for you is to focus time, energy, and effort on knowing yourself. Warren Bennis, a leadership development theorist and advocate, said, "The leader never lies to himself, especially about himself, knows his flaws as well as his assets, and deals with them directly."

Instructions for Human Beings

Let's review what people need from work in a bit more detail and reflect on relevant questions that any leader or business owner should be prepared to answer. Human beings (including the ones who work for you) need these things from you and your organization, no matter if your organization is big or small, private or public, in business, healthcare, education, or any other sector:

- **People need money to meet their basic requirements.** This means that you need to think about how you plan to pay them and what currencies you'll offer in addition to pay. In my hometown of Bend, Oregon, employers consider offering time off during workdays so that employees can enjoy the outdoor playground we live in. From mountain biking on fall afternoons to being the first to ski Mt. Bachelor early on Monday mornings, a currency that matters here, in addition to pay, is the chance to play. *Are you paying fairly? Are you looking beyond pay for what matters to your people? Can people meet their basic needs on what you pay them? What can you offer in addition to money?*

- **People need to do something that matters to someone; they need to contribute.** This means that we need to be able to connect the dots between what we do and something bigger. Every job, from the very front line to the most senior executive, exists for a reason. Mark worked on the line for a speaker manufacturer, and he said that he loved his job despite the tedious nature of the work, because he knew that he was helping people listen to beautiful music, which made their hearts sing. *Are you spending time with your employees to connect the dots between what they do every day and the benefit or impact of that work on someone else? Are* *you coaching your leaders to spend time doing the same?*

- **People need to feel seen, not anonymous.** Being seen means being known. It means that the people we work for and with know our name, and they know what our job is. They notice if we come to work and if we're joyous or down. Recently a CEO client and I were on a walking coaching session, and we bumped into an employee. The employee knew the CEO right away, and when the CEO recognized him and asked how things were going, it was like watching the sun rise. The employee clearly felt valued and seen because his boss's boss knew who he was and cared how he was. *Do you know who works for you by name? Do you spend the time necessary to get to know them in small but vital ways?*

- **People need to connect with other people via real connection.** This is what the Grant Study shows and what Brené Brown's research illuminates: we are hard-wired for connection and we need it as much as we need water. This goes beyond company team-building and beer on Fridays; it has everything to do with whether your organization facilitates and supports the process of forming human connections. The best way to do this is by being real and human, by admitting your mistakes or admitting that you don't know. Nothing, and I mean nothing, draws

"

Nothing, and I mean nothing, draws others closer to us than small acts of vulnerability that reveal our humanity.

others closer to us than small acts of vulnerability that reveal our humanity. *Are you showing your employees what's under the hood? Do you support small intervals in time when the explicit purpose is human connection?*

- **People need to learn and grow.** The need to learn is so basic that in my first book, *Fit Matters*, Cammie and I offered it as an overriding seventh element that encompasses all six other elements of fit. We want to become better, to challenge our thinking and our being in a variety of ways. *As an employer, are you aware of what an employee might want to learn with you? And are you talking about it with them? How are people able to grow or learn at your organization?*

- **People need to feel, and be, safe and supported.** Google's germinal 2015 Aristotle Project validated what many of us already knew: members of high-performing groups at work have psychological safety between them. Psychological safety is "a sense of confidence that the team will not embarrass, reject, or punish someone for speaking up," according to Harvard Business School professor Amy Edmondson (1999). "It describes a team climate characterized by interpersonal trust and mutual respect in which people are comfortable being themselves." This includes being able to feel like an insider, like you belong, even when differences (race, gender, physical ability, nationality, sexual orientation, and more) could make you feel like an outsider. *Do you think your employees feel safe enough to speak up? Do you spend time and effort to create an environment in which listening to each other, and showing sensitivity to feelings and needs, is valued? Do you practice inclusion and model it in your organization, exploring your own unconscious biases and systematic advantage?*

- **People need to be able to make their lives work.** We lead divergent and varied lives. What works for one person may not work for another. Some companies focus on professional athletes as employees because athletes need flexible hours to train, and they need the income. Others make work hours appropriate for working parents. Obviously your organization needs to do what it needs to do, which may mean that employees must flex how, when, or where they work. But a single parent will likely need to be home by a certain time. Or if an employee you value does her best thinking between 7 a.m. and 9 a.m., can you facilitate the end of her shift to be 3 p.m. rather than 5 p.m. so that she can take advantage of her best thinking time without overworking? We can't completely design workplaces around employees, of course, but if employees can't make their lives work around our organizational needs, they won't. *Do you pay attention to the ways in which your workplace supports and enlivens your employees? Do you act in ways that are consistent with the values you profess?*

If you own or manage a company, you should keep in mind, with everything you do, what people need from work. The reasons that we work are many, complex, and often beneath the surface, but they are consistent for most of us. By designing every facet of your workplace around the needs of people, you'll create a Bravespace workplace in which workers can do their best work for and with you.

In Part II we'll examine the five levers for eliminating toxicity in your workplace and creating a Bravespace workplace that's truly fit for human life.

PART III

❧

Creating a Workplace
Fit for Human Life

Chapter 7

୭

Lever I – Who
The Human Essentials

The acquisition of wealth is no longer the driving
force of our lives. We work to better ourselves and the
rest of humanity.

— Jean-Luc Picard

Act I:
Leaders with Head and Heart Habits

As we've discussed previously, leaders who are good for people are essential to creating a Bravespace workplace. My friend Joanne, a research company CEO, said to me, "Sometimes I feel like the people I work with should have trouble walking through doors. Their heads are so big, and their hearts and bodies are atrophied by comparison." She was so right. In my 30 years of consulting, training, and coaching, the vast majority of my clients have been smart and savvy, often with advanced degrees in

"

When we fail to teach heart skills, we inadvertently undercut workers' capacity to tackle the big problems for which they're trained.

technical fields. They're intelligent, educated, and often extremely experienced. So why do they call me? Because my work is about relationships between people in the workplace, something they find challenging.

Over the years I have collected stories that highlight the commonality of people problems at work. A surgery center CEO once told me, somewhat graphically, that he was trained to "cut people," but in his new role as CEO he was being asked to do things for which he was not prepared – to lead, to mentor, to communicate, and to engage partners. The CEO of a small engineering firm told me that his newest engineers were technically excellent, but that the firm was losing projects because of their inability to convey empathy and understanding to clients, who felt that they were working with arrogant and "thick" technicians. The number of stories like this – the tech company that flops because its coders are unable to collaborate, the architect whose buildings are beautiful but whose clients don't feel valued, the retail shop owner who can't seem to keep her staff for more than a few months – is astounding. These examples show an atrophy of what I call heart skills – the people in these stories are technically fit for their jobs but they lack skills such as self-awareness, social awareness, and emotional intelligence that would enable them to lead, inspire, partner, and create change.

Part of the problem is that the educational approaches of traditional science, medicine, business, engineering, or technology programs don't focus on developing heart skills (empathy, vulnerability, transparency, compassion, courage). When will our academic and professional systems and processes stop growing human beings with great big head skills and small, atrophied heart skills? We fail doctors, teachers, engineers, MBAs, architects, managers, and technologists when we don't arm them with a complete set of tools, one that includes activating emotional pathways and emphasizing relationship-building skills. When we fail to teach heart skills, we inadvertently undercut workers' capacity to tackle the big problems for which they're trained. Fortunately, this oversight in education keeps me employed, but I would like to see students and employees alike demand and seek out education that goes beyond the technical.

The Four Pillars of Heart-Based Leadership

This book is an attempt to give leaders the tools that deepen their heart skills in order to help them lead. In this chapter I identify and elaborate upon four theoretical pillars of heart-based leadership that, although tricky to master, will enrich and deepen relationships between leaders and their followers.

To begin, though, I want to step away from the stories of failure and use an example of an extremely successful leader to identify those four traits of effective heart-based leadership. I was in the audience of an international conference, one I'd been attending regularly for more than a decade, where the focus was on bringing together disparate members of one trade. This year there was an uneasiness among the attendees, though, because the president of the hosting organization wasn't there. Unknown to most, he was experiencing unforeseen and serious medical issues. He had never missed the conference before, and he was eager to make an appearance. During the conference closing ceremony the team decided to live-cast him onto the screen of the conference plenary to share a few words. When his face came on the big screen, however, his planned address vanished before he could begin, drowned by the roar of a standing ovation.

He was obviously shocked at this response. As I watched I could see the emotions on his face: humility, profound gratitude, awe, admiration, fear, and patience. Looking around the audience I saw faces that seemed to say, "We've missed you and we're so happy to see you. Things were working without you, but your absence has weighed on us and we want you back."

This audience was obviously a group of people who were willing to follow their leader anywhere. What makes some leaders so compelling to their followers? The incredible leaders I have met, like this one, point to four pillars of heart-based leadership:

- **Emotional Stirring.** The first pillar is one I call *emotional stirring.* As the story above shows, there's an emotional connection between strong leaders and their people. As humans, we're drawn by feelings of joy, belief, gratitude, wonder, even fear and recovery. Data and logic help us solve problems and get results, but it's emotion that draws us toward a leader, gets our attention, and makes us listen. We become captivated by our hearts, moved to unexpected expression, and compelled to seek out that emotional stirring again. Inspiring leaders know that emotion isn't something they must get out of the way before getting the work done but is, rather, the core drive that fuels their team.

- **Authentic Vulnerability.** The second trait I call *authentic vulnerability.* The leader on the live-cast

"

Inspiring leaders know that emotion isn't something they must get out of the way before getting the work done but is, rather, the core drive that fuels their team.

"

We'll do anything for leaders who strive for greatness through and with their imperfections.

showed his followers his fear and gratitude; likewise, the constituents, by way of their applause, expressed their genuine appreciation and admiration of their leader. When leaders show their imperfections, we see them as real and human, and our trust grows. Our tolerance for showmanship, veneer, and ego dancing is very low, and such patterns turn us off from real engagement. Leaders who can be vulnerable reveal their courage and their trust in their followers. We'll do anything for leaders who strive for greatness through and with their imperfections.

- **Compelling Belief.** The third trait is having a *compelling belief*. Leaders need a reason to be in the lead. A leader exists for those moments when the way is unclear, or the task seems insurmountable. In the case of this leader, he articulated his clear belief in the industry's unity and a deep appreciation of difference in his mission to unify a global trade. His ability to set forward an ambitious, clear, and compelling future for the conference's constituents inspired hope in the participating members. The ability to return to that belief, even when the community was unsure and hesitant, drew followers in and kept them engaged.

- **Harmony Between the Words and the Music.** The fourth and final trait of heart-based leadership is *harmony between the words and the music.* The words are what we say, and the music is the feeling we give others. Dissonance between what we feel and what we hear erodes trust. If leaders say they're hopeful, we want to feel the emotional vibe of hope. If they're anxious and concerned, we want to see that in their faces and understand where that comes from. In this leader's face, on screen, it was clear that his fear and his hope lived simultaneously and captured the dynamic nature of their changing industry as well as his heart. Humans are skilled at reading subtle, nonverbal communicative cues, and they know when someone is faking. This fourth trait requires leaders to know what they are feeling, and to express it in a

❝

Humans are skilled at reading subtle, nonverbal communicative cues, and they know when someone is faking.

way that's consistent and aligned with what we feel emanating from them.

With these four pillars of heart-based leadership in mind – emotional stirring, authentic vulnerability, compelling belief, and harmony between the words and the music – I'd like to look at some stories that demonstrate the various ways in which different leaders embody them. This section is intended first to give you an intuitive sense of what this type of leadership looks like, and then to offer tools that you can use to develop heart-based leadership in your Bravespace workplace. In what follows I will combine my experience with recent research perspectives on profound, heart-based leading.

Leading from the Heart

The CEO of a large medical system demonstrated this quality beautifully during a difficult time for the organization. There had been a violent incident in which a patient accosted a staff member with a knife. Police were involved, and although no one was badly hurt, it was traumatic for all. When the team convened after a press conference about the situation had been resolved, the CEO thanked everyone for their courage and perseverance and visibly became emotional about the moments of terror. She simultaneously expressed gratitude, fear, and confidence, which together contributed to her remarks drawing the staff toward her leadership even as she was authentically impacted.

For context, consider that our sense of what it means to be a leader evolved from the Northern European ancestry of the earliest European immigrants to North America, and it's sometimes called "white male culture." For many white men, who don't think of themselves as a group, the notion of having a culture is new, but this European background shapes modern business culture in many ways. The inclusion leadership firm White Men as Full Diversity Partners (and Principals Bill Proudman and Michael Welp) describes some definitive traits of this culture:

- A survivor mentality that focuses on the future
- A tendency to rugged individualism
- A can-do attitude
- Motivations stemming from intellectual principals of conscience
- Focus on hard work, action, and task completion
- Striving toward growth and materialism
- Measured moderation and silent strength
- Focus on status and rank over connection

These cultural characteristics are so ancient, familiar, and embedded in our notions of how business works, that it may be hard for us to recognize them in ourselves; we may simply see them as "leaderly." When I say this, I don't mean that all white men lead with this mindset, but the practice stems from the cultural practices of groups of white men. Anyone (white, male, non-white, female, etc.)

who grows up in the primary culture will naturally assimilate this mindset.

In the culture of women, who remain an outsider group in the world of work when it comes to leadership, ownership, and funding, we learn and are encouraged to manifest the qualities that John Gerzema and Michael Dantonio (2013) discovered are critical for global leadership in the future. They discuss these traits in their longitudinal study of over 10,000 people, *The Athena Doctrine: How Women (and the Men Who Think Like Them) Will Lead the Future*:

- Connectedness
- Candor
- Empathy
- Openness
- Vulnerability

- Humility
- Patience
- Trustworthiness
- Flexibility
- Balance

But most women in the workplace don't lead with these traits, for the same reasons that men in the workplace don't. It's more common for white women at work to assimilate the dominant business culture, which values authoritarianism and decisiveness. White women, who have advanced more than other outsider groups over the past 30 years in the workplace, still don't have parity in power and authority at work. And women of color are even further behind. Many women, like me, know that the best way to be heard and seen in work circles is to look and act more like men: decisive, direct, action-oriented, independent, and data-driven. To me the process of dumbing down my feminine leadership qualities seemed a reasonable thing to do after countless exchanges with others in which I was regarded as too emotional, too open, too focused on collaborative wins, and too soft. Yet at the same time, women experience pushback from others, as I have, about our adoption of the more "masculine" traits – we're too pushy, we're bitches.

Things are changing in the realm of leadership, and, as Gerzema and D'Antonio discovered, effective leaders will embrace leading with their hearts as well as their heads. In order to do so, leaders need to know themselves, and they need to know themselves well.

Critical Self-Reflection

A grad school professor of mine, Ed Tomey, once told me that the two questions we must ask ourselves as leaders are "Who am I?" and "Who am I with you?" Although these questions are short and simple in form, the answers are neither short nor simple.

I'm 56 years old, and answering these questions is no easier now than it was when I was 22. Sure, I have a better understanding of my flaws, my skills, and my desires, but I still frequently step in familiar dog doo as I navigate the many personal and professional worlds in which I live and work. For example, although I spoke briefly of socialized gender roles above, I can easily hear the protests of my male audience members – "What do you mean 'white male

"

We interact, we affect each other, all the time in every way, whether we mean to or not.

culture'?" Or the disagreement of people of color, who may have had vastly different experiences navigating the work world. Even as I strive to understand the nuances of what makes a leader effective and to share what I know, I might inadvertently offend or be misunderstood by others. I'm as likely to make mistakes in my interactions with others today, with familiar behavioral gaffs or attitudinal biases, as I was when I started my career.

Part of the impact of these two questions is that the answers to them walk the line between, on the one hand, the pragmatic dogma of business ownership and citizenship and, on the other hand, the spiritual basis of motivation and passion. For example, when I ask myself, "Who am I?" I encounter, in my professional capacity, my ambition, curiosity, helpfulness, and optimism. But I also see the other roles I fill: mom, partner, sister, co-worker, and caregiver. Asking myself, "Who am I with you?" can help to clarify these roles. With my clients I see my gift of optimism, the gift and danger of my high energy, and the vulnerability inherent in depending on others. This second question invites me to consider each of the people in my life constellation, and their dreams, their wounds, and their connection to me, in ways that make our partnerships purposeful and important, rather than random. We interact, we affect each other, all the time in every way, whether we mean to or not.

We are human beings, hard-wired for connection, and as a result, we're inextricably tuned in to cause and effect with one another in everything we do. Asking, "Who am I?" in the realm of partnership, isn't a complete question when it's not paired with, "Who am I with you?" Knowing yourself, as a leader, will facilitate an honest expression of your needs, wants, and motivations. It creates the critical pathway for empathy and listening, and it should be the starting point for leaders on the path to making their companies Bravespace workplaces.

Making Mistakes (Yes, Leaders, Too)

Being alive means being imperfect. And yet many of us relentlessly work to hide our imperfections, as if they're separate from us. Doing so creates cultures of comparison,

"

Knowing yourself, as a leader, will facilitate an honest expression of your needs, wants, and motivations.

in which we're frightened and watch others for evidence that we're good enough, or close to perfect. Brené Brown (2010) has studied and clarified the dynamics of imperfection and speaks poignantly about mistakes as part of our story: "Owning our story can be hard but not nearly as difficult as spending our lives running from it. Embracing our vulnerabilities is risky but not nearly as dangerous as giving up on love and belonging and joy – the experiences that make us the most vulnerable. Only when we are brave enough to explore the darkness will we discover the infinite power of our light." Paradoxically, when we as leaders show up as real and imperfect, people are drawn to us, and when we hustle to appear as if we have it all perfectly together, people keep their distance.

This paradox of being worthy and flawed at the same time is a dynamic I have seen with my clients and roles as a leader at many levels. I know, for example, that no matter how airtight I make my schedule I will miss a meeting, pick

"

Paradoxically, when we as leaders show up as real and imperfect, people are drawn to us, and when we hustle to appear as if we have it all perfectly together, people keep their distance.

up my children late, or miss a deadline. I hate it when I make a familiar mistake. But part of what it means for me to lead well is to acknowledge my mistakes. In the situations in which I work I often see leaders who unwittingly send the message that mistakes are unacceptable, despite our knowledge that they're inevitable. What does it take for a leader to make graceful mistakes?

Here are six tools that I've been practicing so I can handle my mistakes well:

- **Listen to my intuition (really listen) and act on it.** Those times when I've ignored what my gut is telling me almost always have played out badly. Shutting down my own natural responses is in fact shutting down my emotional connectedness, my intelligence, and my wisdom born from experience. Why would anyone want to do that?

- **Have compassion and empathy, for myself.** I am naturally skilled at empathy and truth telling with others. Uttering words of care, love, tenderness, forgiveness, and compassion to myself are ways I can walk my own talk, and when I do it authentically it helps. I find it much harder to speak compassion to myself that I do showing genuine empathy for another person.

- **Remember that others are imperfect, too.** Nobody else has the secret recipe for being perfect, so I can let myself off the hook for being imperfect. When did I get the notion that others have all this life stuff figured out, and that I didn't get the memo? There is no memo, and my world of entrepreneur, mother, wife, friend, consultant, etc. is more whirlwind than tidy, and there are no instructions.

- **Notice the things that trigger me to feel shame, which is key to my leadership practice.** Brené Brown describes shame as the internalized belief that we're not worthy of love and belonging, and she says that when we're triggered into shame, our brains are in survival mode. Usually nothing good comes of it, so it's important that I stop myself from feeling shame and not engage in overblown self-flagellation. I can and should stop just short of the cliff edge, before my feeling of shame is triggered, because when it's triggered, I start hustling to protect myself, and hustling to feel worthy is never pretty, rarely real, and feels awful.

- **Remember that adventure has been my friend always, and that big risks open big possibilities.** I have, since I was a little girl, pushed myself to extreme pursuits – acting, mountaineering, whitewater rafting, horseback riding, starting a business. I know the benefits of just jumping in. When I make mistakes, it's often because I'm trying hard, living big, and putting it on the line. My colleague Mei Ratz says it this way: "Nervous means do it."

"

Comparison is a prevailing curse of western society in general and women in particular, and it leads to a whole sequence of bad results.

- **Know that comparing myself to others is a bad idea.** Always. Comparison is a prevailing curse of western society in general and women in particular, and it leads to a whole sequence of bad results. Let's stop comparing ourselves. Comparison is especially dangerous for leaders, because employees need to be regarded as unique individuals, and for what they uniquely bring to work.

Mistakes have a place in the practice of leadership and at work. Making small errors along the way allows us to avoid catastrophic mistakes when it really counts. Mistakes are essential to how we learn and to the learning process, but they're never easy. Bravespace workplace leaders make the effort to model a tolerance for imperfection, and they see it as part of learning and innovating. By doing so they invite the people who work for them to take risks and to learn. People are drawn to these leaders because they know that they can show up fully, as they are, and be seen and contribute, even when they're less than perfect.

Leading with Heart is Leading

The stories I've told so far are just some of the ways that I've seen leaders express the four traits of heart-based leading. Effective heart-based leaders spend time and effort cultivating relationships. They treat their role as a leader as a practice, not a destination. They craft agreements that honor the unique nature of everyone who works for them, and they ensure that people feel seen. They speak what's true, even when it's damn hard, intimidating, emotional, or scary.

Heart-based leaders acknowledge that emotions are important for what we do at work; they're not a private excess that we need to hide. Heart-based leaders lead from the heart (feelings) as well as from the brain (ideas and knowledge.) They show vulnerability as a means to authentically connect, and they're willing to take the first step. Heart-based leaders know that people come to work every day wanting to connect and contribute, and they remember, even when the going gets hard, that their employees are people, not machines.

These leadership practices are essential first steps in creating Bravespace workplaces. I have distilled the points from this chapter into the following list. Post it on a wall, and figure out what each point might mean for you today, next week, and next year. And in Act II of this chapter, we'll examine the other human essential, teams who care.

ACTIONS FOR CREATING BRAVESPACE WORKPLACES
Leading from the Heart and the Head

Note: The toolset I recommend for everyone is Dare to Lead, a research-based approach built by Dr. Brené Brown, which contains a tangible set of tools and skills for leaders to develop in building their courage practice – essential to showing up and leading. I am honored to utilize this work as a Certified Dare to Lead Facilitator, and there are others with that designation who can help you.

For Leaders or Business Owners

- Learn about emotions: yours and theirs.
- Develop a courage practice by being vulnerable and going first.
- Elevate the heart (feelings) and practice empathy.
- Walk your talk (including talking about your imperfections and mistakes).
- Give time for real connection at work.
- Ask yourself, "Who am I?" "Who am I with you?"
- Match your words to your music (feelings).
- Get feedback from your people with surveys or pulse checks or conversations about how you're doing.

For Employees

- Talk to your supervisor about how connected you feel to them (or not).

- Learn about difficult conversations and have them.
- Think of feelings as a source of data and share them with an open heart.
- Practice empathy.

For HR or People Development (if they exist in your company)

- Create tools for regular performance and brave and connecting conversations for supervisors.
- Move away from ratings and rankings (they don't work); focus on frequent conversations.
- Define programs for leader learning, including practice at heart skills.
- Give leaders feedback on their relationships.
- Hold senior leaders responsible for being brave.

"

Heart-based leaders acknowledge that emotions are important for what we do at work; they're not a private excess that we need to hide.

"

Leaders who go first with
emotional honesty and
transparency potently model their
own essential humanity, paving
the way for others to follow.

Act II:
Teams Who Care

THE WORST TEAM I WAS EVER ON just didn't get me. They hired me, and I was thrilled. It was a cutting-edge technology company, and I was eager to show them my stuff. What I experienced when I got there was demoralizing. There was no room for my strengths and weaknesses; I felt that all I had were weaknesses. What made it even worse was that my peers seemed to be experiencing success after success. Our meetings were a game of one-upmanship. My colleagues' projects were all completed on time and on budget, while mine, which weren't going as well, became the focus of every meeting. "How can you do better, Moe?" It wasn't long before my optimism and energy had eroded to frustration and anxiety. I changed from eager and curious to fearful and secluded, merely following a to-do list, my creative spark gone. It didn't take long for me to search out and happily

TEARS AT WORK

In Bravespace workplaces people use heart and head, self-awareness is encouraged, mistakes are regarded as lessons, and emotions can run high.

People often tell me that they worry that tears at work will make them appear weak, and that when someone cries in their presence, they don't know what to do to help. Tears make us uncomfortable in different ways. Women are afraid that they'll be regarded as overly emotional if they cry, while men who cry are often either teased or celebrated for their vulnerability.

We often assume that crying equates to sadness, but, says Ad Vingerhoets, a psychologist at Tilburg University, tears are often correlated to feelings of "helplessness, hopelessness, and the lack of adequate behavioral responses to a problem situation." Something stressful happens, or we feel humiliated, and the tears come. As human beings, we have a limited range of ways to express intensity of feeling, and crying is one of them.

Tears are a data point. When someone is crying, it indicates that something important is going on inside of their emotional realm. Noticing this, and working to sort through the complexity of feelings, usually leads to progress in a conversation or situation. Viewing tears as important information, rather than as a shameful occurrence, helps us to normalize and utilize the gift of feeling.

Tears at work, as in the rest of life, are an act of vulnerability. When we tear up or cry at work, we're showing up and being real. So, if someone cries at work, it's an invitation for connection, because that person is showing the vulnerability of authentic presence. Crying is an effective way for some people to move through emotions. We *will* stop crying. As any parent knows, even babies eventually stop crying.

Tears at work are evidence that we're human: tender, soft, and open. Leaders who go first with emotional honesty and transparency potently model their own essential humanity, paving the way for others to follow. On a team, the presence of tears may draw a group together with deeper understanding, compassion, and care for the needs and interests of one another.

We don't shame or ostracize one another at work for laughing out loud, or angrily expressing frustration. Crying is simply one more very human, very real, very tender aspect of our humanity, and it has a place at work along with other relevant emotions.

"

Tears are a data point.

commit to another firm. Back then I didn't know what made teams click, so I assumed that I was the problem.

In my work I see countless individuals thinking the same thing. "My job sucks, and it seems like it's all my fault." I'm here to say that it's *not* always your fault. There are teams that work and teams that don't. In this chapter I'll combine research, a whole lot of experience, and Act I's strategies for heart-based leading, and take a close look at what makes a team brave and how you can help your team to thrive.

What Makes a Good Team?

The elements of an effective team have been studied extensively over the last 75 years. Early researchers believed that teams just got better over time. This can be seen in Bruce Tuckman's model (1965), where teams naturally progress through predictable stages (forming, storming, norming, performing). More recent models, such as Patrick Lencioni's (2002), understand that team health takes a bit more work than mere patience. Lencioni asserts that vulnerability-based trust is a keystone of healthy team development.

Google's Aristotle Project (Rozovsky 2015) and Thomas Malone's MIT research (Wolley and Malone 2011) can

"

Mistakes have a place in the practice of leadership and at work.

126

be consolidated into three common characteristics of high-performing and healthy teams.[2] The first characteristic is equal airtime: groups that solved problems well together paid attention when someone spoke and shared the time in roughly equal amounts, with no one person dominating. Relatedly, the Aristotle Project revealed the importance of psychological safety: people weren't fearful of harm or recrimination when they shared, so they took more risks and those risks were supported by the group. The second is social sensitivity: the members of groups that performed well were in tune with each other, noticed subtle shifts in mood and demeanor, and were alert to and responsive to one another's needs. Third, Malone's research showed that the teams that performed best with complex problems contained more women. This may be because women are socialized more toward the feminine values – connectedness, empathy, trustworthiness, balance, etc. – discussed in Gerzema and Dantonio's *The Athena Doctrine* cited earlier.

My own work affirms these findings. Healthy teams are the ones whose members clearly share a mission and listen to and appreciate one another. I work with teams desperate to reach this level of success. What I often see are teams that try creative things such as bringing cupcakes on birthdays, kegs of beer on Fridays, or hosting

---

2. In Malone's research, individual IQ and aggregate IQ had no effect on a group's ability to solve complex problems, again suggesting that teams need heart skills and not head skills.

events such as fire walking or team paintball. While these activities can be fun,[3] they usually don't deepen the relationships of the team members in the heart-based way that healthy teams need. One problem with these sorts of events is that they often alienate the introverts in the group, who might find socializing exhausting. Another is that they tend to lead to superficial connections at best. As business leader and best-selling author Margaret Heffernan (2015) says:

> Social capital [the ability of a team to grow the trust, knowledge, and shared norms that make healthy groups] isn't about chumminess. It doesn't mean work colleagues have to become best pals or that good cheer is a permanent requirement. Many of the greatest teams are scratchy, sharing impatience with anything less than the best. Grumpy orchestras tend to play better than cheerful ones; they're focused on performing better, and happiness is the output, not the input, of their work together. In organizations with high degrees of social capital, disagreement doesn't feel dangerous, it is taken as a sign that you care; the best-thinking partners don't confirm your opinions but build on them. They know that every idea starts out flawed, incomplete,

---

3. Gallup's research (2017b) suggests that having friends at work is one of the top 12 contributors to job satisfaction, but a healthy team environment is less about being friends (socially) than about being able to relate to others in a way that makes us feel seen and connected.

"

When team-building activities aren't designed with the intent of building team health and developing social capital, they flop, leaving people happy for the cupcake, but no closer to increasing the health of their team.

or downright bad. In organizations with high degrees of social capital, conflict, debate, and discussion are the means by which it gets better.

When team-building activities aren't designed with the intent of building team health and developing social capital, they flop, leaving people happy for the cupcake, but no closer to increasing the health of their team. Leaders of Bravespace workplaces instead foster team health by intentionally fostering brave teams. That is, teams need to study what makes a good team generally, but more importantly they need to reflect on what makes the members of their teams thrive. Reflecting on the next four big questions around trust, conflict, team dynamics, and courage will help your team develop their social capital and become that grumpy but effective orchestra that Heffernan envisioned.

Is There Trust in Your Work Situation?

The dynamics of a workplace can often interrupt the formation of vulnerability-based trust. Competition that pits employees against each other insures that they'll look at each other suspiciously. These types of environments, where trust and respect don't exist between colleagues, almost always work out badly. Politics, power mongering, competition, and subtle discounting behaviors degrade the faith and confidence of colleagues and create hidden and/or public tensions.

The evolution of healthy work relationships is proportional to the trust and mutual respect that are nurtured between people. When we feel connected, we feel safe, so we're willing to be vulnerable, so we courageously speak our truth, which elevates others' ability to trust us – and the cycle perpetuates itself. In trusting relationships, we can make mistakes, learn, and grow, without fear of judgment or recrimination. In the workplace, the presence of trust between colleagues is a key element of team cohesion.

Look at this list of traits common to highly trusting teams – teams composed of people who have invested in creating positive, healthy, trust-based relationships at work – and ask yourself which you see at your work and which you don't:

- Individuals talk openly about their strengths and their weaknesses.

"

When we feel connected, we feel safe, so we're willing to be vulnerable, so we courageously speak our truth, which elevates others' ability to trust us – and the cycle perpetuates itself.

- People offer both support and challenges in meetings, clarifying their intentions and asking questions without appearing judgmental.

- People know more about each other than just their names.

- People are seen to be valuable beyond their output. Maybe there are references around the office to people's lives outside the workplace (images, artwork, etc.).

- People assume positive and generous intentions in their interactions with one another.

- Competition is focused on winning in the market or against the competition rather than internally. When we win, we win together.

- Team leaders and people managers walk the talk – they do what they say should be done.

- In meetings, sharing and listening are distributed evenly.
- People admit to their mistakes and discuss their learning opportunities.

The presence of vulnerability-based trust is the baseline for all the work that brave teams can accomplish together. Bravespace workplace leaders spend the time and effort to teach, model, and practice with their people how to bake trust into all interactions that teams have with one another, every day.

Does Your Team Engage in Healthy Conflict?

Unhealthy conflict saps a workplace. What's more, the shrapnel of unresolved conflict can stymie, stunt, and stop the work at hand. The ability of people at work to move from conflict to resolution is a key determinant of team health. Conflict, when we work through it, is a positive thing. It opens the possibility of extreme growth. Healthy conflict invites innovation, inspires creative problem solving, sows hope, and deepens trust. In dynamic, healthy workplaces, people disagree, have ideological differences, and confront divergent points of view, and they do so with their heart skills. Some essential elements that are present in conflict-healthy workplaces include:

- People challenge each other's ideas in meetings without hesitation because they know that this challenge will be regarded as the challenge of an idea

"

Unhealthy conflict saps a workplace.

and not the judgment of a person. Issues are left on the table until they're resolved and all participating parties are satisfied.

- When people disagree, it's done with respect.

- People tell the truth, even when it's hard. They are vulnerable.

- Leaders model healthy conflict with their colleagues and with their teams.

- There are no gossipy "meetings after meetings" because people are forthright with their feelings in the moment.

How Big is Your Team?

Copious research confirms that productivity is highest in teams with four to twelve members (Brodzinksi 2014). Teams with fewer than four members end up functioning more like partners, without the desired synergistic lift of team cohesion and elements such as innovation, feedback, creativity, and productivity. On the other hand, teams with more than twelve members become unwieldy. Big teams see communication breakdown, disengagement, and division into nonfunctioning subteams. Based on my own experience working with hundreds of teams over the last 30 years, I'd say the sweet spot is between eight to twelve members, with fluctuations allowable.

Although size matters when creating impactful teams, it's secondary to establishing a team purpose; clear guidelines and expectations for individual contributions; ongoing, team-focused investment and feedback; and a defined leadership structure.

How Courageous Are You and Your Teammates?

Working in a small, trusting, conflict-healthy team is scary. People often cite fear as the central struggle when it comes to having difficult conversations at work. Their thoughts include, "I don't want to hurt them," "I fear offending them," or "I don't want to alienate them and lose the relationship." Even when we know the benefits of honest feedback – healthy conflict, innovation, creativity, and deepened trust – the fear of either being hurt ourselves or hurting the receiver often causes us to avoid or dilute the important message we have.

Adapted from the work of Gordon Barnhart (2018), these four types of courage can help us remain centered and focused during difficult conversations:

- **Courage to See and Speak the Truth.** Before we can have a difficult discussion, there must be something to discuss. That is, we must foster the courage to see the (often difficult) truth. Once we see it, we can name what's happening between us. By learning to see and speak the truth, we can mend problems or create new solutions. Being a truth teller means authentically verbalizing what we see to others, despite our worry that it might offend. It helps to remember that the truth we speak is what's true for us – the other person may not see it that way.

- **Courage to Create and Hold Forth a Vision of the Desired State.** This form of courage invites us to imagine ourselves and the other person successfully on the other side of the difficult conversation. Holding an image of getting through the conversation intact and in strong partnership can guide the conversation. With a vision of a positive outcome, our fears are less likely to usurp and break down the conversation. It can also be a good way to articulate intention. Don't look at where you are, but where you want to go. If you have a successful resolution and an even stronger partnership clearly in mind, and you don't let fear guide and derail the conversation, positive outcomes are more likely.

- **Courage to Persevere and Hold the Course.** The intense feelings that arise during a difficult conversation can threaten the entire interaction. We must hang on even when the interaction gets stormy, trusting that on the other side of our differences is a successful resolution wherein we understand each other and feel that we have honestly expressed ourselves, listened, and been heard. A mindfulness practice that teaches discipline of the mind and patience in uncomfortable situations can aid in one's ability to persevere.

- **Courage to Collaborate with and Rely On Others.** Ultimately, difficult conversations are conversations: they're an interaction. If we're in a feedback exchange or difficult conversation with another person, it's because both of us matter to the outcome – the partnership itself is consequential to the eventual outcome. We have each contributed to the problem and the solution. Telling ourselves that we can do it alone usually results in the failure to garner and offer the support we need to do an excellent job. Our ability to foster interdependence creates an environment in which we can accomplish phenomenal things.

Developing these courageous habits in your team can encourage the development of healthy feedback and ways to communicate.

Listening to the Music

Live music performed well is the ultimate example of team performance in action. Annually, my husband and I head up the road to the Sisters Folk Festival, an event in our home community that showcases musicians from around the world. Inspired by these artists, I have made a list of the top five things you can do to create a Bravespace workplace that will move your group from *barely getting by* to *achieving amazing results together*:

1. **Listen first.** Great musicians watch and listen to one another acutely. As they start to play, someone goes first, and the others fill in behind based on what they hear and what's needed. When someone decides to do a riff, or change a scale, the others are tuned in to catch it and respond instantaneously. Although some take the spotlight, they are enabled to do so by their bandmates. *In the teams you work with, are you listening to the others? Do you listen first to try to understand? Or are you so busy with your own work that you fail to notice the others at all?*

2. **Know your part.** Some musicians pluck, some bang, some blow – each voice, each instrument, and each player has a specific contribution to the whole that is, in fact, the point. *In your team, are you crystal clear on what your part is? Do you know what it takes to give your best performance to the team? Do you have the self-awareness to know what your greatness looks like and how you can deliver it repeatedly to your team?*

3. **Be vulnerable and imperfect.** I once saw a singer performing a new song. She was eager to share it and proud of it, but because it was new, she needed

to use her iPhone to recall the lyrics. She took a big risk in trying something new, and she was honest with herself that it would be best if she sacrificed the appearance of professionalism for a genuine performance of her new song. It was a beautiful song.

Putting yourself out there with your sound, your voice, and your ideas requires an awareness that it may not be perfect, but it will still be right. If this musician hadn't performed out of fear that she might forget the lyrics, we wouldn't have heard it. If team members never risk, teams stay predictable, static, and slow. *What is scary for you to say to your team members? What ideas do you have that you hold back from sharing? What might happen if you jump in and take a risk before you have it all perfectly worked out? What tools can you use to help manage your fear so that you can take risks bravely?*

4. **Have a plan.** Musicians on stage invariably have a song list that they follow, that little slip of paper they tuck under a drum or in their pocket that reminds them what the plan is for the set. The band knows the plan and has rehearsed the flow in order to be ready to perform each song in order. *Does your team have clarity on why it exists? Do you each know what the outcomes are and what the timing is? Can every member tell you on any given day how the team is progressing?*

"

Planning doesn't always cut it.

5. **Be willing to go off plan.** Planning doesn't always cut it. Take the young songwriters I saw who unexpectedly joined a seasoned expert, or the musician who plucked a violin when his mandolin broke, or the time the audience was unexpectedly asked to sing the refrain and created a magnificent harmony with the lead singer. *Are you willing to vary from the plan with your team when something comes up? Can you discard your solid plan when it doesn't work and be nimble and responsive in the moment?*

At some point in our lives most of us are fortunate enough to experience what true team cohesion feels like, yet thinking deeply about the part we play in making this happen is often relegated to off-time and accidental reflection. Take time to listen to the music. Notice how talented artists can come together to create the ultimate synergistic lift and cohesion. Identify your part and the many other parts that align to create powerful teams that can achieve the phenomenal.

Bravespace workplace teams spend time and energy fortifying their individual and collective partnership skills.

##

Bravespace workplace teams
spend time and energy fortifying
their individual and collective
partnership skills.

They know that what they each know is less important than
what they know together, and their priority and focus remain on the success of all.

Now that we have explored Lever I, Who – Human Essentials, let's examine the next powerful element for creating a
Bravespace workplace, Lever II, What – A Conscious Culture.

ACTIONS FOR CREATING BRAVESPACE WORKPLACES
Teams Who Care

For Leaders or Business Owners

- Note that not all work groups are teams. Does your team share a common purpose? What is it? It's usually better to invest in teams where there's a compelling and specific reason to partner.

- Create an environment of safety by having shared norms for how the team members behave together, including how they share airtime. How will you tell each other when one of you has talked too much?

- Design ways to invite vulnerability. Ask people to share mistakes that they've made. Invite personal stories that help team members to see one another in richer ways.

- Go first with vulnerability. As the leader, what you do goes a thousand times further than what you say they should do.

- Commit to occasional rest and play. It creates resilience.

- Invite and practice healthy conflict.

- Ask personal questions that probe at the emotional underpinnings of decision-making. Instead of asking, "What problems do you see with this plan?" ask, "What about this plan makes you uncomfortable?" "Why?"

- Turn up the dial on feelings: name them, share them, and validate them with empathy. Sharing and making room for the emotions at play between people helps them to feel safe and tune in to one another.

- Host occasional team advances,[4] in which you and your team celebrate, play, plan, and connect. These are best when they're away from the office and when they inspire or delight in any small way.

For Employees

- Know yourself, your role, what makes your heart sing, and what your best qualities are for any team on which you serve.

- Learn about difficult conversations and have them. Notice the things that you're feeling but not saying. Say those things.

- Invest time in developing relationships with your colleagues through genuine connection.

- Think of feelings as a source of data, and share them with an open heart.

- Practice empathy.

---

4. We prefer to use the term *team advance* rather than the traditional *retreat*, which wrongly suggests going backwards.

For HR or People Development (if they exist in your company)

- Offer tools that help teams to start off well, such as designed experiences, kick-offs, assessments, or team advances.

- Point employees back to their peers when they come to you with complaints or issues. "Have you and Sue tried to sort this out? If so, have you tried . . . ?" Help them to work it out themselves.

- Offer programs that build skills to have difficult conversations. Train your people in heart-based leadership.

- Support leaders in maintaining team health.

- Require the senior team to be brave.

- Survey more often, using pulse survey tools such as Waggl, Survey Monkey, or any tool that allows you to frequently get the inputs of your employees about how leaders and teams are doing.

Chapter 8

ॐ

Lever II – What
A Conscious Culture

*Wake up. True change demands action, not passive
acceptance. There is deep beauty in being strong, in
being fearless. There are no mountains high enough.
Be awake. Be mindful. Create the life you want to live
and live that life, not the ones other people want you
to conform to. Be the change. With each action, each
thought, each word, each intention.*

— Angela Davis

I WAS IN MAINE THIS SUMMER, visiting a lifelong friend
and her daughter. My friend likes to take naps. During
one of them I took her daughter and mine to a local thrift
store, left them there, and took myself out on an ice cream
date. Ice cream store culture is familiar to me – I grew up
eating and working in one on Cape Cod (the infamous 4
Seas Ice Cream.) The shop I found on this recent day took
me right back to that summer job.

"

Organizational culture is like the air we breathe. We don't always feel its presence until it changes.

It was cool inside. On the walls hung family portraits, and it smelled like sweet, fresh, homemade ice cream. Even more than those material similarities, what I noticed was the culture of the business. The layout was a bit confusing, so when I entered, I stood around, unsure if they waited on the tables or if I ought to order from the register. White I was hovering the owner caught my eye and asked, "Would you like to enjoy a treat here or take one with you?" He was inviting, efficient, and kind. I told him two scoops of the double chocolate for here would delight me. The chocolate was on the other side of the store, so he asked an employee to get it. She seemed willing and happy, and double-checked my order politely. I was caught by the ease and efficiency of these two. What I felt was the carefree bliss of a child, out of school for the summer, spending her precious pennies on an ice cream cone. As I sat and enjoyed my cone, I continued to watch this little team. It was clear that the way they did things carried the energetic ease that I felt.

Maybe you've had a customer experience like this one – you enter a store and can immediately feel something about it. Sometimes those experiences are negative, maybe a sales-person is too pushy or a customer service agent a bit impatient, or maybe those experiences are positive, like the one I described. We call this feeling at work "culture" and it defines, simply, how we do things here.

Organizational culture is like the air we breathe. We don't always feel its presence until it changes. It encompasses the way that things are done at an organization, and it impacts the feeling of a workspace, for customers and employees, in a big way, for two key reasons. First, organizational culture determines an organization's ability to sustain its health over time via performance and results, and second, it shows employees and customers what the experience of working with that organization is like, whether the employees bring their best to their work. Culture is easy to break but hard to fix.

I'd like to start by addressing four factors that invariably create an unhealthy work culture. Notice if any of these traits are true of your organization, because they can point to some things that need to change.

Four Surefire Ways to Mess Up Your Culture

- **Espouse one set of values while practicing another.** You can have pretty, glossy values statements posted all over your organization's walls, in the employee manual, and tattooed on every leader, but if your organization's day-to-day practices fail to match these values, your employees and your costumers will notice. Your company will no longer be trusted. Take the manufacturing company that advertised a safe working environment but hadn't updated their safety procedures to match their new equipment. This company's actions didn't match their stated values. Instead of feeling safe, employees got the message that what this company really valued were the increases in production that resulted from the new machinery. Act in accordance with your values, every time.

- **Tolerate employees who fail to practice the organization's stated values.** Leaders don't always initiate company culture, but they certainly contribute. I can't tell you how often we've discovered pockets of managers within organizations who completely undermined the stated cultural values. Their employees knew it, their customers knew it, and even the managers involved knew it.

  One organization that I worked with claimed in posters on the walls that their culture was one of "inclusion and relentless communication." Yet this same company continuously rewarded a senior VP who almost always failed to involve his team, communicate accurate information, and practice partnership with any of his colleagues. No matter what the organization said about how they did things, this leader didn't model it, and the employees' faith and confidence in the culture was fragile.

Deal with your managers who haven't bought in to the company culture. Hold them accountable and recognize (through compensation, training, or other means) the importance of their roles in creating company culture. Expect them to contribute positively and to embody the organizational culture in their everyday actions. If they can't or won't support the culture, replace them with someone who can and will.

- **Have two cultures: One for customers and one for employees.** Employee experiences are customer experiences. I had an experience with an airline attendant that showed what happens in an organization that fails to connect the dots between how they treat their employees and how they treat their customers.

  My booked flight had been canceled, so I went to the customer service desk to get another booking. The agent, to quote her more or less, said, "Ma'am, I totally understand what I can do to fix this problem and get you where you want to go, but I'm not authorized to do those things. I suggest that you call the 1-800 number to see if the agent you reach has the authority to fix this for you."

  This agent clearly knew that treating me well as a customer mattered and that solving problems was her job. She wanted to help me, and she knew that her company promise was to help me. But the level of authority she was given limited her ability to help. The dissonance was astounding, and I felt bad for her, bad for me, and bad for the airline, which that day lost my trust as a costumer.

Treat your customers and your employees consistently.

- **Assume that company culture will take care of itself.** As I mentioned earlier, organizational culture appears as this nebulous, "felt" quality of an organization. As such, it can be easy for leaders to think that if they put the right ingredients into their organizations, a healthy culture will emerge. A company I worked with once had implemented some suggestions they had received about culture, including having beer kegs at work on Fridays and doing personality tests on all its employees. However, they failed to regularly discuss and demonstrate the qualitative elements of the culture they valued (informal professionalism, self-knowledge, work hard/play hard) in their day-to-day work, so employees found the leadership behavior to be inauthentic and rote.

  Company culture is something that can be measured, learned, taught, and changed. I've often been called into an organization that's transitioning from founder to growth stage, but the culture isn't transitioning. Most companies start because someone has an idea or an invention, and they assemble an organization to bring it to the marketplace. The company forms itself around the personality habits and quirks of the founder, who is often more inventor than leader. Over time the culture of how they do things grows to emulate and reinforce how that founder or leader liked to do things. This may work in the early stages, but as people join the company the resultant accidental culture often becomes problematic. A founder who values innovation, for example, may not encourage a culture of consistency. A founder who rules by hierarchy alone may not encourage collaboration.

Deliberately deciding how you want to do things in your organization ensures that the culture you end up with serves your goals and mission. Culture is difficult to build, which is why it needs dedicated focus.

These four, sure-fire ways to mess up your company culture all have something in common. They each show a dissonance between the underlying beliefs of an organization and the day-to-day practices of an organization. Edgar Schein (1985), a noted theorist of organizational culture, has a taxonomy of terms that are quite helpful in diagnosing where these dissonances might occur.

In Schein's framework, the most surface level of culture manifests itself in what he calls the *artifacts* of a company:

things that can be seen and felt by an observer, such as facilities, offices, rewards and recognition, titles, policies, attire, slogans, creeds, and published mission/vision statements. Much press has been created in the past 20 years about company perks that all boil down to artifacts: on-site day care, coffee lounges, dry cleaning services, or nap rooms. While these perks seem meaningful to employees initially, research suggests that, in time, these external perks are less important than intrinsic rewards, such as success in a role, rich and fun connections with other people, feeling part of something important, and learning. "Nearly nine out of ten, or 86 percent, of Millennials (those between the ages of 22 and 37) would consider taking a pay cut to work at a company whose mission and values align with their own, according to LinkedIn's latest workplace culture report," according to CNBC (Meija 2018). While these perks are nice, company culture – that felt presence of an organization – runs much deeper.

Schein called the second level of organizational culture the *professed values*. Unlike a mission statement, these are the values expressed through the *behaviors* of the organization's members. In an organization with healthy culture, professed values and the written company values are often similar. The professed values often lurk unnoticed, but they're apparent in the way that an organization works. Whether implicit or explicit, those values become evident to employees during their work.

Underneath and informing the professed values are what Schein calls the *tacit assumptions* of the people in an organization. Team members, often unconsciously, tailor their actions to their tacit assumptions. These assumptions are sometimes called the unwritten rules of a company, and they explain why there can be paradoxical behaviors within the organization.

It's often the tension between professed values and tacit assumptions that makes orientation and assimilation to a new company a slow and arduous process for new employees. During this time they are unwittingly working out the differences between what is professed and what is done, which informs the employees' beliefs about what matters.

As an antidote to the negative examples above, here are three stories that showcase organizational cultures whose three levels are synchronized. In particular, look for these four elements: 1) leaders leading their organization's culture in addition to the mechanics of the business, 2) values at the center, 3) integrity between how things are discussed with employees and how things are done with customers and clients, and 4) transparency, with purpose and no secrets.

- **Story One: Good Customer Service.** On a recent flight an error was made in my itinerary and I ended up in somebody else's seat on a full plane. I was told to get off the plane, which was the last flight of the day, and walk back inside to the desk where they would remedy the situation. When I got to the desk, I was told the plane I'd just been on had left and that I would have to travel home the next day. I was unhappy about this. The representative who was helping me quickly noticed my agitation and made a call to the plane. She grabbed my paperwork, spoke privately to a colleague, and walked me back down the people carrier. In 10 minutes, I went from feeling annoyed and angry to feeling supported, seen, and cared for by the airline. I could see that the woman helping me was gratified at having been able to give me the assistance she did. She was able to do so because she was comfortable seeking assistance from a higher-up because she knew it was for my benefit as a customer.

- **Story Two: Support and Appreciation.** Years ago, I applied for a line of credit for my business. The first bank I approached was a large chain where we had all six of our family accounts. I was told that I needed my husband to co-sign for a business line of credit, even though he was uninvolved in the business. I declined because my husband had absolutely no affiliation with my business, and walked down the street to a then-new local bank. The manager invited me to a small room and asked how he could help. I told him my story, and he listened, making notes.

I walked out with my first robust line of credit and a new bank, feeling supported, valued, and appreciated. The manager was clearly motivated to meet my needs, which was his mission. He had a solution, and he knew how to access it. He was empowered, had clear authority, understood how to get something done quickly, and empathized with what I needed as a future (and now very loyal) customer.

- **Story Three: Collaboration, Information Sharing, and Empathy.** A client of mine recently suffered a small car accident on her way to work. She was on her way to an important meeting and called her boss to say she was delayed because her car needed to be towed. Her boss immediately expressed concern for her welfare. "Was she hurt?" "Did she need help?" And then her boss provided reassurance that the meeting would be covered by her colleagues. Because of their team approach, my client wasn't the only person in the know, and the meeting went off flawlessly. Collaboration, information sharing, and empathy were not only company values but actual company practices. When an emergency arose, the company was prepared to handle it.

These successes weren't caused by employees' stand-up desks, free movie passes, nap breaks, unlimited coffee supply, or other surface elements of culture. The people

"

Rather than focusing time and money on surface elements of company culture, leaders of Bravespace workplaces invest their resources in the development of people practices that sustain healthy culture.

involved acted the way they did because they had been trained, encouraged, and indoctrinated into a culture that manifested its values, such as customer focus, accountability, team orientation, and problem solving. These employees understood, consciously or not, the central tenets of the organizations they worked for and knew how to do their work according to these tenets.

Rather than focusing time and money on surface elements of company culture, leaders of Bravespace workplaces invest their resources on developing the people practices that sustain healthy culture. Usually this means spending time and money on training, communication, management, and leadership development. Instilling confidence and belief in the core values of an organization, and helping people to connect the dots between these values and the things they do every day, is what drives strong company culture. Here's how to do it:

- **Study your culture.** As the felt quality of an organization, culture often lurks under the surface and takes explicit searching out. Remember that culture is driven by the beliefs, values, and assumptions held by the people who work there. These beliefs, values, and assumptions drive behavior. Look for symbols, rituals, actions, and behaviors, and ask what those tangible practices reveal about a company's culture. This process should reveal both the natural strengths and weaknesses of the company.

  Leadership teams who take the time to either measure their culture with a valid assessment tool, asking employees how they do things, or otherwise openly discuss the beliefs, values, and assumptions that drive behavior in their organization, can realistically assess the often invisible and ignored dimensions of culture that matter.

- **Talk about culture.** Whether you measure or simply try to name your culture, it's important to engage every employee, to find out what they feel and notice about how the company does things. Since culture is a product of the shared beliefs and assumptions of employees, discussion about culture at all levels helps an organization to more specifically connect the dots between what they do today and how they want to be tomorrow. Dissonance between espoused beliefs and values and those in practice becomes a potent lever for change. It's essential that all employees be engaged in these conversations, rather than just the team at the top, since change will require all employees to begin to think differently in order to act differently.

- **Take focused action to change.** Interestingly, most companies we work with want to start here, at this final step. Before change can happen, you need to know the root causes and the culture that exists. Revisit the previous steps.

Pick one to three things at a time to change that will make a difference in your organization's culture. Focus allows all employees to practice new ways of doing things. Trying to consciously rewire tacit assumptions may not always work at first, but highlighting key practices and behaviors that express those assumptions does.

Here's how one group of leaders does it. During their reflection, this team found that employees were often keeping silent as a result of pervasive low trust. The leaders wanted to grow the trust that existed in their workplace and create a less fearful culture. Together they committed to bring more heart-based work to how they accomplished things together, as well as how they led their teams. In working to build their new leadership team, they have successfully been able to target specific ways to walk their talk and

"

Culture is the lifeblood of every organization.

create vulnerability-based trust at all levels. People can engage in ideological debate that's healthy and constructive, which increases performance and job satisfaction.

For example, the leaders now start team meetings with a quick check-in on how people are feeling. They consciously share with one another the problems or challenges they're facing, and the mistakes they've made. They also make it a point to share with the employees the reasons behind the decisions that have been made, practicing the transparency that leads to trust.

This team bravely examined their culture, talked to all their employees about their specific ideas and hopes, and were then poised and ready to act.

Culture is the lifeblood of every organization. It derives from the assumptions we make and the beliefs we hold, and it drives our actions. Bravespace workplace leaders consciously create a culture that mirrors and matches their values. Use the ideas below for action in your organization.

Next, in Chapter 10, we'll examine Lever 3 for creating a Bravespace workplace, Where/When – Purposeful Design.

ACTIONS FOR CREATING BRAVESPACE WORKPLACES
A Conscious Culture

For Leaders or Business Owners

- Study your culture and put it into words.

- Measure your culture; there are a variety of effective tools in the marketplace.

- Share the results with employees and talk about what it means to them.

- Consider yourself a cultural petri dish: whatever grows inside of you will grow in your company. Do what you say you want done. Show up. Be real.

- Expect your leaders to walk the talk, and hold them accountable when they do things that are inconsistent with the culture.

- Share how you deal with your vendors and partners. Watch how they do things, and make sure that their culture and yours align.

For Employees

- Participate in culture assessments and be honest.

- Consider yourself a cultural ambassador: spread the word.

- Speak up when you see people acting in ways that undermine the culture.

- Think about what you do to contribute to your company's cultural health.

For Human Resources or People Development (if they exist in your company)

- Find the right tool(s) so that your organization can measure regularly.

- Make it your job to keep culture in front of the leadership.

- Don't think that you own the culture – it's not yours alone.

- Examine how what you do represents your company's culture.

- Make yourself more a cultural steward than a compliance officer.

Chapter 9

~

Lever III – Where / When
Purposeful Design

Indifference towards people and the reality in which they live is actually the one and only cardinal sin in design.

— Dieter Rams

THE WHOLE EVENT WAS THOUGHTFULLY DESIGNED. I had arrived in downtown San Francisco to give a talk and do a book signing at a tech company. From the minute I walked in the door, it felt like home. Someone met me cheerily at the elevator. As the representative of my hosts she said that they were excited to have me, and she whisked me into the cafeteria/auditorium where I would be speaking. My books had been lovingly arranged all around the little elevated stage, around which people naturally congregated. There were pens, full of ink, sprinkled everywhere and balloons in the corners. Someone put a lavaliere mic on my shirt and quickly adjusted it. I smelled something in the

163

air, and my host said, "Would you like a fresh doughnut?" The welcome they gave me made me feel that I was meant to be there at that moment to talk to those exact people. It felt this way because my hosts had carefully designed the event around my needs, my audience, and my book.

We live in a designed world today. Coe Leta Stafford (2018), the managing director of IDEO U, the educational offshoot of global design company IDEO, describes human-centered design as the attempt made by organizations to focus on the people they serve. For Stafford, this process "leads to human-centered products, services, and internal processes." What makes design important is this human-centeredness. Design thinking asks how we can design this system, space, or product in a manner that facilitates human well-being and prosperity. In this chapter I'll talk about what it means to design workplaces that are fit for human life – Bravespace workplaces – by focusing on accountability, time, and the physical structures of an organization.

I use the words *space* and *place* differently. Place identifies the many felt components of work – the calendar and scheduling systems, how people communicate, the culture and vibe, the practices, the energetic atmosphere of the organization. Space, on the other hand, refers to the physical location of work – the building, the layout, the wall color, and so on.

Leaders of Bravespace workplaces take design thinking concepts and apply them directly to how work unfolds in four key categories:

- **People:** How are people organized in your organization?

- **Time:** When do your people work? (work hours/flex time)

- **Location:** Where do people work?

- **Impact:** How does your organization impact the communities in which it lives?

How to Organize People: Intentional Structure

It's very rare that a problematic person in a workspace is malicious. More often, problems between people at work stem from the way that an organization is structured from top to bottom.

Typically, we think of organizational structure as the boxes in an organizational chart, but that merely represents the formal structure of a company, the first layer of the onion. The actual structure lies in how accountability flows through the organization. We use accountability to make and maintain agreements at work. "I need to do this because if I don't, I'll be held accountable by others." This is different from responsibility, which is our internal sense

"

It's very rare that a problematic person in a workspace is malicious.

of drive and motivation. "I need to do this because I want to succeed."

Think of it this way. I like to run and walk. Over the years my friend Sandy and I have run or walked thousands of miles together, often in the early morning. I do it for fitness and for connection (we talk while we walk), and because I want to. But many times, before the sun comes up, especially when it's raining, I'm tempted to send a quick text to Sandy, "Sorry. Can't make it." What keeps me from doing so is that a) we agreed to meet, b) she's waiting, and c) I know that if I don't show up, she'll tell me that my flakiness left her hanging. I do what I should do because I feel accountable to Sandy. When organizations have "people" problems, those problems are often accountability problems.

Canadian psychoanalyst, social scientist, and management consultant Eliot Jacques (1990) advanced a theory of stratified systems that maintains that when accountability isn't clearly named in the contract between an employer and an employee, both fail. Jacques put it this way: "One of the most widespread illusions in business, namely, [is] that a company's managerial leadership can be significantly improved solely by doing psychotherapeutic work on the personalities and attitudes of its managers." He maintained that "properly structured, hierarchy can release energy and creativity, rationalize productivity, and actually improve morale." In order to do our jobs well – work we're proud of and want to be seen – we need to clearly understand what doing a job well looks like, and to whom we're accountable for doing the work.

In her most recent book, *Dare to Lead*, Brené Brown writes that for courageous leaders, clarity is kindness. Being clear in Bravespace workplaces is kind. Lack of clarity is unkind. And yet the management fad pendulum tends to swing right and left from militaristic hierarchy to chaotic open-team approaches, with very little data to tell us which systems work best for kind clarity.

Most companies organize themselves organically, at least in the beginning. A founder or owner has an idea, they start selling stuff, and then when they need to, they add people. It's a naturally occurring process, and it usually works fine right up until it doesn't. The tipping point varies, but in my experience it's often when an organization gets to be around 100 people or $5 million in revenue. Often the wheels come off the bus because the number of people reaches a volume where communication across and within functions becomes unwieldy. The system goes from one in which many people share knowledge and access, to one in which not everyone knows what they need to know.

Accountability should be assigned so that every person knows what they need to do and can focus on those things. This is best measured, according to Jacques, by understanding the complexity of a task and the time that it takes to complete it. For example, a jewelry design company with 95 employees needs at least a few people to make sure that what needs to happen today is happening (FedEx comes, shipping is received, customers are supported), as well as someone to think ahead to next year ("What product line will launch in what channels?"), and even a few people to consider the multi-year window ("Will we outgrow our space?" "Is manufacturing going to need to be outsourced?" "What if silver costs go up?").

Although the work is daunting, it's not overly complex. It's critical that every employee in your organization be able to answer two questions:

- **To whom am I accountable?** In this age of matrixed organizations and collaborative, cross-functional partnerships, we tend to resist single-person accountability. Yet the simplicity and reliability of single-person accountability cannot be overstated. I can work with many people day in and day out, but it's important that I know to whom I must report my successes and failures. If I'm accountable to too many people, I can find a way of skirting my responsibilities by manipulating whom I report to. We need one person at work to whom we're accountable.

- **What does "doing a job well" look like?** To know if we're doing our job well, we can track both qualitative and quantitative specifics. Nonetheless, despite nearly 80 years of HR-driven rating and ranking approaches to performance management, we have no evidence that employee rating and ranking systems improve people's performance. According to professors Peter Cappelli and Anna Tavis (2016):

> One *Washington Post* business writer called annual performance ratings a "rite of corporate kabuki" that restricts creativity, generates mountains of paperwork, and serves no real purpose. Others have described annual reviews as a last-century practice and blamed them for a lack of collaboration and innovation. Employers are also finally acknowledging that both supervisors and subordinates despise the appraisal process – a perennial problem that feels more urgent now that the labor market is picking up and concerns about retention have returned.

What are the implications for Bravespace workplaces? Hopefully, the result is more frequent, more compassionate, more honest, and more rigorous person-to-person conversations about how things are going than we have had in the past. People learn in different ways on the job, and the career paths they'll take in the workplaces of tomorrow are hard to predict. In the future there will be jobs that we can't imagine today, and it's predicted that people will have twelve to fifteen careers in a lifetime, so performance and development depend on personal, meaningful conversations between managers and employees about where they're going.

These conversations will facilitate what Deloitte (Buckley and Bachman 2017) describes as a "series of developmental experiences, each offering a person the opportunity to acquire new skills, perspectives, and judgment." Careers in this century may follow an upward arc, with progression and promotion at various times, but they'll look nothing like the simple stair-step path of generations ago.

Consider When We Work

A potent currency in today's workplaces is the ability to flex work hours. Although most businesses are open from 9 a.m. to 5 p.m., we all have a time that's best for us to work and get things done. For me, it's between the hours of 4 a.m. and 7 a.m. My brain is most alert at that time, and I feel capable of anything. On the other hand, mid-afternoon I generally start to drag. But no matter when we may be most productive, we live in a world of schedules imposed on us by others – shops, schools, children, flights, and so on.

One of the most significant demands on people's work schedules is taking care of children and parents. Schedule conflicts at work tend to increase when children are involved, and these conflicts can vary with their ages and individual needs. Greater family demands – more children or adult dependents at home – frequently create a need for more flexible or less-demanding work conditions. Job requirements that an employee once enjoyed or tolerated, such as weekend hours or extensive travel, can suddenly create significant stress. Traditionally women have carried the burden of juggling work with family, and while that's still true to a great extent, men are increasingly taking on more responsibility at home instead of sacrificing their personal lives to their jobs' demands.

Flexible schedules work well for many of us because they enable us to clearly distinguish between time at work and time in other roles. These are my work hours, and these are my life hours. Other individuals prefer integrating work and family roles throughout the day, maybe trading text messages with our children from the office or monitoring emails at home and on vacation rather than returning to work to find hundreds of email messages waiting to be dealt with.

Another time factor for many individuals is how long it takes to commute to work. As people become busier, time becomes increasingly valuable, and every hour counts. One study conducted by Canada's University of Waterloo (Hilbrecht et al. 2014) concluded that people with the longest commutes have the lowest overall satisfaction with life. The authors report that commute lengths are linked to a

"

A potent currency in today's workplaces is the ability to flex work hours.

> "
> While the stress of competing obligations is increasing, our willingness to make personal sacrifices for work is decreasing. As workplaces realize this, norms, expectations, and practices are changing.

sense of time pressure. People who spend the most time on the road experience higher levels of stress because they constantly feel hurried. Many of them spend much of their time on the road worrying about all the activities they're missing.

As workers demand more flexibility, work is structured more broadly. We're seeing less of the "enterprise shift" (9 a.m. to 5 p.m.) as more and more employees move to adjunct or "gig" situations, often primarily to meet their lifestyle needs. In the United States, more than 40 percent of workers are now employed in alternative work arrangements, such as contingent, part-time, or gig work, and this percentage is steadily rising, increasing by 36 percent in just the past five years (Agarwal et al. 2018). Some workers today aren't satisfied with traditional nine-to-five work hours; they prefer to schedule their work around hobbies, caregiving, and other aspects of their personal lifestyles. These changes place new demands on employers.

While the stress of competing obligations is increasing, our willingness to make personal sacrifices for work is decreasing. As workplaces realize this, norms, expectations, and practices are changing. When these conflicting demands compete for our finite time and emotional energy, our work and our other relationships and responsibilities suffer as well. In a study conducted by Barry Posner and Jim Kouzes (2010), 50 percent of managers agreed with the statement, "Anxiety about my job frequently spills over into my home and personal life." In a study by researchers Danielle Talbot and Jon Billsberry (2010), 68 percent of the participants mentioned that their families, other social networks and connections, or obligations to their communities affected their fit at work. Changing societal norms, such as the influx of women into the workforce, the increased prevalence of dual-earner couples, movement away from traditional gender-based roles, and technology that blurs the line between work and personal time, all contribute to the challenge. When you add factors such as the tremendous growth in the number of single parents and employees taking care of aging relatives, lifestyle challenges affect all of us.

Leaders of Bravespace workplaces need to figure out how people's work times affect the business. For some companies, such as those that deal with customers, academic

"

We need to feel safe and equipped for success in our workplaces – out of the elements, with the tools we need to do our job, and with adequate light, air, and temperature control. Beyond that, the physical requirements for workspaces vary greatly, and individual taste for comfort, beauty, design, and privacy are highly subjective.

institutions, and medical facilities, the need to be open during specific hours requires workers to be at specific locations at specific times. But for many others, work can be done anytime. And, in fact, the work will likely be better if work times and places can flex to fit employees' natural rhythms, needs, and habits.

Consider Where We Work
(Remote, Home, and Space)

Offices are changing. The ambience of a work location is becoming increasingly important, motivating some companies to do away with traditional cubicles and glass-partitioned offices. Many employers are spending copious thought and energy to design places for their employees. Sometimes the efforts seem over the top, such as Amazon's Spheres, three connected park-like glass domes, three to four stories high, in downtown Seattle. The Spheres house tens of thousands of plants, hundreds of species – virtual jungles. But "unlike most jungles, the Spheres are a workspace. Banks of tables, secluded meeting nooks and benches strewn throughout the complex can seat up to 800 people. Amazon envisions the building as a change of pace for its workers, a place to 'feel differently, to think differently,' said Ron Gagliardo, the Spheres' lead horticulturist." (Day 2018)

Efforts like these have yet to prove effective at making a workplace fit for human life. Noble attempts to design places to match values, including the open-office concept, where everyone from the CEO to line staff works in the same bullpen environment, sometimes fail. Many people report that open offices increase isolation because people wear headphones all the time to create their own private space, blocking out distractions and thereby interacting less than they did when they had separate offices. There are numerous studies that explore the relationship between the physical space of a workplace, business performance metrics, and what employees value (Gensler's Workplace Index, The Leesman Index, etc.), but the results vary.

We need to feel safe and equipped for success in our workplaces – out of the elements, with the tools we need to do our job, and with adequate light, air, and temperature control. Beyond that, the physical requirements for workspaces vary greatly, and individual taste for comfort, beauty, design, and privacy are highly subjective.

Leaders of Bravespace workplaces approach physical space and ergonomics with a thoughtful mindset about what their employees want and need. What kinds of human interactions are required to get work done? Do workers interact with customers? Should leaders be visible and accessible? Is there a need for privacy?

Since office design, furniture, and ambience are often costly, the Bravespace workplaces I have seen have had their workplaces consciously designed to enhance and support the work that needs to be done and enable people to thrive. For example, one of my clients had a delightful workspace that consisted of simple modular offices attached to a barn. What made the space special was that it was easy and comfortable for staff to move between the barn and the offices during their workday. The facility was a therapeutic riding program, and the indoor barn, where most of the staff spent most of their time, and where services were delivered, was the most critical aspect of a healthy and vibrant workspace. But the staff also needed desks, computers, and phones, which were kept in the modular offices, which, while clean and quiet, were far from fancy.

Many workplaces don't need (or want) employees to come to work at their location. Organizations can simultaneously reduce overhead and offer remote work as a benefit to employees. The primary drawback for remote workers is the loss of interaction with colleagues and the chance to synergistically connect with other people for ideas and dialogue. Bravespace workplace leaders design ways for remote workers to meet and connect with other people at work occasionally, as a supplement to time on the phone and video conferencing.

Remember that Workplaces Live in Communities

Workplaces plunked down in neighborhoods with little or no concern for who also lives there have a negative effect on locals and on workers. For example, workers who must commute long distances to work rarely linger after work, so they don't get to know or benefit the local community or economy. This hurts companies in the end, because when they need talent, they can't find it locally. The difficulty in recruiting people for trades today is likely a direct result of a decrease in the felt impact of a company to the locals. If high schools in areas that hire trades offer no training, apprenticeships, or incentives for local young people to join a local company, the business cannot hire the talent it needs. This puts more strain on the existing workforce to work longer hours, making workers feel overwhelmed. The perception that there are no jobs locally drives young people to move away.

Remote workers can benefit from being part of communities of workers using local, shared workspaces. It's why shared workspace providers such as WeWork and The Riveter have proliferated. In shared workspaces, small companies and independent workers can benefit from camaraderie and partnership, reducing feelings of isolation.

The Myth of Work-Life Balance

For many people, the goal of designing a workspace is work-life balance, an ephemeral notion that's at the center of designing workplaces fit for human life. Work-life balance is regarded as a harmonious unity between when and how one works and when and how one lives. This balance is often talked about in terms of a schedule. Work-life balance, some say, looks like this:

7:00   I wake up naturally with the sunlight, fully rested after nine hours of sleep (yeah, I go to bed at 10:00).

7:15   I read my gratitude journal over fresh-pressed, organic French roast.

7:45   I go to the gym, where I do the workout that fits perfectly into the yearlong training scheme that was last year's New Year's resolution.

8:45   I shower, dress, and enjoy my bike commute (the reason I moved).

9:00   At work I attend a few meetings. They are joyful, and I feel grateful to work with people who feel like friends. I also sink into some focused creative production.

12:00   I eat the nutritional (and delicious) lunch I prepared last night.

5:10   I bike home, taking the long way to enjoy the setting sun.

6:00   I eat a fully satisfying dinner with my partner, read my children bedtime stories, and write in my gratitude journal.

8:00   My partner and I have an open, easy, rewarding conversation (something we practice a lot), make love, and drift off to sleep right on time.

Ah, the balanced day – time for work, play, connection, and self-care.

Of course, I've never experienced a day like this one. My days, and, I suspect, many of yours, consist of periods of intensity and chaos, energizing hard conversations, just-in-time reports rushed to the post office, meetings prepped for and noted, an occasional collapse into a Netflix binge, sometimes a yoga class or a delightful novel. Regardless of what my days look like on a calendar, very little about my life *feels* balanced as it is happening. The felt quality of my days is much more dynamic – at times I'm transfixed and fully occupied in what I do; at others my mind wanders and I wish I were elsewhere. I'm constantly weighing tradeoffs and compromises, punctuated by delight, brilliance, mess, and sweat.

I often feel guilty that my life doesn't match the images I have of the perfectly balanced life. I feel deeply inadequate when I have to reschedule an obligation or adjust my expectations, admitting to myself that I can't do it all. These feelings billow into an anxious fear that I've become a workaholic, someone who is unable to stop obsessing about work.

At other moments, though, I recognize that work-life balance doesn't have to match how I feel. In these moments I have the clarity and courage to say to the world, "Look! It's working! This dance, the wildly out-of-balance, CEO-mom-sister-wife-mother-friend-former-athlete-wanna-be-creative-writer dance, is moving to the music! Somehow, my business is working, I have people who love me, and what I do is making a difference somewhere." These moments of gratitude, amid the felt chaos of my life, feel like a third option, between perfect balance and workaholism.

I have a few role models who seem to live the same way. Michelangelo worked for days on end when he was painting a fresco that he loved. My architect father was always sketching in his book – on vacation, in the kitchen, at dinner. When we love what we do, it becomes us, fully, completely, and powerfully. When the work is worth doing, we don't mind doing it. We're lucky to have those moments when the clock stops, and we lose awareness that this is "work." Employers should bottle up those employee moments as an asset.

Bravespace workspaces recognize that work has a natural place in our lives. It expands and contracts according to the needs of the employer and the employee, and it's important to monitor the impact of the ratio of work and life on the health of both the individual and the organization. If we want to work hard sometimes, we should! No guilt, no shame. It feels good, matters to the world, and gets things done. And we should remember, while we work, that rest and play enable us to grow.

Now that we are grounded in three key levers for creating a workplace fit for human life (Who – The Human Essentials, What – A Conscious Culture, and Where/When – Purposeful Design), let's explore Lever IV – Meaning and Context in Chapter 10.

ACTIONS FOR CREATING BRAVESPACE WORKPLACES
Purposeful Design

For Leaders or Business Owners

- Think about the flow of accountability as you solidify your structure, and put people in roles accordingly.

- Remember that how far ahead your workers have to think and how complex that thinking needs to be affects the healthy flow of expectations between managers and employees.

- Thoughtfully decide when people work, and make sure that you understand and can explain the context of those decisions to your workers.

- Make your space (offices, shop, etc.) match your culture.

- Consider the communities in which you operate and be part of them.

- Have frequent, honest, and wholehearted conversations in your workplace about what "doing a job well" looks like and how things are going. Banish ratings and rankings.

For Employees

- Make sure that you understand the needs and expectations of the company you join when it comes to work hours, work location, and flexibility, and make sure that these requirements fit into your life.

- Ask the hard questions when you feel that your company is out of sync with what they said when you started working for them.

- Participate in open, two-way performance conversations to learn and to make sure that you're meeting expectations.

- Try to associate with other people at work, even if you're working remotely, to build a real connection with them.

- Be a community citizen by caring for the workplace you inhabit as if it's your own.

For HR or People Development (if they exist in your company)

- Assess the company's structure at regular intervals to make sure that the accountability flow makes sense and is working for everyone.

- Banish rating and ranking systems. Find a human-friendly way for employees and managers to talk about what "doing a job well" looks like and how the work is going.

- Consider peer-to-peer feedback mechanisms. We care a great deal about what our colleagues think.

- Challenge leadership to invest in leadership and team learning and development instead of overspending on surface perks.

REMOTE EMPLOYEES
How to Stay Connected

Every time I travel I meet people who do the most amazing things in a home office, traveling occasionally to be with clients or colleagues in person. The age of interconnectedness leaves us wondering how best to manage the unique dynamics of remote workers. Distances vary from a few blocks to a few continents.

Companies large and small leverage technology to assist in remote partnerships. They use sophisticated video and teleconferencing features to facilitate the ability of employees to see and hear each other in real time. Additionally, frequent travel, email, and on-line communication tools allow people to share information, outputs, decision-making, and tactical progress.

But even with all these aids that allow people to work together across distances and time zones, people are often frustrated because they don't feel connected to one another. What do they mean by this? If their work outputs are clearly defined, and progress is easily traceable, why do people not feel connected with one another? And, more importantly, how can this problem be remedied?

What people miss is the authentic, emotional connection that's so easy to establish when they're face-to-face with one another, having informal interactions, and passing in the hall. Daniel Goleman, Richard Boyatzis, and others use the term *resonance* to indicate a dimension of emotional intelligence relating to the ability to become attuned to one another, often on an unconscious, subliminal level.

SUGGESTIONS FOR REMOTE WORKING SITUATIONS

- Preserve and prioritize time with remote workers for pure connection, not just project status, updates, and details.

- Ask questions of one another, such as:
  - "What's new with you?"
  - "What success are you proud of this month?"
  - "What's getting in your way of success these days?"
  - "How are you feeling about our interactions and the clarity of our roles?"
  - "What are you looking forward to next?"
  - "How's your family?"

- Take a portion of planned video or phone meetings to offer non-tactical, personal connection.

- Use applications such as Skype and Google Hangouts as an alternative to phone calls and computer multi-tasking in order to establish a visual connection with one another.

Remember that establishing an emotional connection takes intention more than it takes time. Five or ten minutes of mutual investment in the partnerships that matter can bridge the gap far more efficiently than reams of emails and project updates.

Chapter 10

∂

Lever IV – Why
Meaning and Context

*The greatness of a community is most accurately
measured by the compassionate actions of its members.*

— Coretta Scott King

Why Do You Work?

EVERY DAY, most of us make a choice to get out of bed,
get dressed, commute (or don a headset), and pass our
day working. We go to work even when we don't want to.
According to Barry Schwartz (2015), author of *Why We
Work*, "Ninety percent of adults spend half their waking
lives doing things they would rather not be doing at places
they would rather not be." Why? We all have our reasons,
and the first to roll off our tongues is often "because I have
to." In a capitalist society such as ours,[5] we need money to

---

5. Note that the phrase *to spend one's time* directly implies that time operates
like money. It also implies that time is finite, that we only have so much of it.

take care of ourselves. In the modern age we trade our time, effort, skills, and experience for cash and other benefits. But, Schwartz notes, it comes down to a higher purpose. Indeed, in my research for *Fit Matters*, we identified meaning – knowing that what we do matters – as one of six essential elements to a great work fit (Carrick and Dunaway 2017). Which makes sense. As humans, we seek meaning everywhere. So if we commit our lives to working, we seek meaning from the work that we do.

Workplace research seems to confirm this claim. *Fast Company* (Poswalski 2015) reported that "more than 50 percent of Millennials say they would take a pay cut to find work that matches their values, while 90 percent want to use their skills for good." We seek ways to matter. But for many of us, meaning at work is missing. According to the Centers for Disease Control and Prevention (Smith 2013), four out of ten Americans haven't yet discovered a satisfying sense of their purpose. Nearly a quarter of all Americans don't have a sense of what makes their lives meaningful.

In every job held by a human being, a connection to work that's seen by others and makes a difference is important. No matter how entry-level the work, we simply feel better when we think that the effort we're making makes a difference to someone. It can be as simple as a supervisor who notices the extra effort we put in, or a CEO who gives us accountability and room to innovate.

When I talk to clients about this, they sometimes look at me as if my head is upside down. Especially if they make things. "Moe, we sell (insert any object), so our mission is to sell more of it." Got it. But when I say meaning, I don't mean that it is always necessary to save the world. I mean that you should offer to the people who work for you at least one of the following aspects of meaning or purpose:

- **Feeling Seen (I bring something unique, related to me).** Feeling seen means that employees feel that their organization cares about them. Not generically, simply as the person with the training and experience to do a job, but as a unique person with a name and a unique synthesis of qualities and insights that will add unique value. Our human need to belong is tightly connected to feeling seen at work. In Bravespace workplaces the people who work there are seen for who they are, in even small ways. People know each other's names. Employees can hang pictures of their beloved people on their walls. Managers give feedback regularly to their employees that helps them to learn and lets them know that their effort is noticed.

- **Feeling Necessary (What I do matters to someone and has an impact).** I had a client tell me the most devastating story. A new worker at a small manufacturing plant was injured the first week he was on the job, and he was sent home. He had to miss six weeks of work. During that time only one person called him: the HR person who was processing his workers' compensation paperwork. This made him feel like a number in the system. It got worse when he returned to work – no one at the front desk knew where he worked or who his boss was. They asked him to wait in the cafeteria while they sorted it out. No one ever came. He went home, somehow received a paycheck for 12 more weeks, and sought another job. My client, a leader of this organization, only heard this story when the worker called the HR department to tell them to stop paying him because he felt guilty taking money when he wasn't working.

Time and energy is spent in Bravespace workplaces to make sure that every employee, from Day 1, knows where they fit in the organization's ecosystem. They understand why the work they do matters to the organization overall, and what the impact would be if they weren't doing their job.

- **Feeling Occupied (I feel busy and engaged).** Engagement is a popular buzzword for organizations. It serves as a measure of the extent to which employees feel connected to and stimulated by the company they work for. Have you ever had a job where you watched the clock tick minute after minute? The odds are that if you have, you were barely there. When we feel occupied, the time flies by. And when we don't, we find ourselves surfing the web for job openings, fantasizing about better opportunities, and seeking other projects. We find meaning in our jobs when we feel fully occupied by the work at hand.

Bravespace workplaces are designed to make sure that people have enough to do, most of the time. Employees are actively encouraged to think broadly about what they should focus on so that they stay busy and thinking.

- **Feeling Compelled (The organization's products and mission are meaningful to me).** More and more often, people are looking to hitch their wagon to a company that feeds their value system. They don't want to work just anywhere. A company that has a higher-order purpose, that contributes to the world, be it socially, environmentally, or with an innovative product that makes lives better, draws employees who connect to that purpose, and that connection keeps them there longer.

Simon Sinek (2009) speaks about this dynamic in his popular book and TED talk, *Start with Why*. He says, "If you hire people just because they can do a job, they'll work for your money. But if you hire people who believe what you believe, they'll work for you with blood and sweat and tears."

Bravespace workplaces have leaders who think about why the organization exists. And those leaders translate the purpose of the organization to the role of every person who works for them. Not just once, but often, in a variety of ways.

I consulted with a client who was a small, drywall-corner manufacturer. The head of the company asked the salespeople to bring videos from the field to HQ to show the office and line staff what it looked like when their products were used in buildings. These short clips of condominiums and art museums all over the country that were beautiful and built safely had the employees who never left their location jumping for joy at their contribution to making the world better.

I will always remember the boss who showed me, when I was15 years old, what a difference a fresh, hot cup of coffee made to the customers who came to our café on their way to work. And the supervisor for the janitorial job I had when I was 19, who conveyed clearly to me the importance of cleaning hospital rooms thoroughly, so that patients didn't get more ill from their hospital stay. In both those instances, I felt that I was making a contribution to something, that my efforts made a difference to someone.

The Sanctity of Work in Bravespace Workplaces

My mother, my sister, and I have an expression. Sometimes when we're grumpy about having to work on a particularly hard day, we say to each other, "Ah, the sanctity of work. Remember, it's better than the alternative." This is true on so many levels:

- **Work gives us a way to contribute.** Human beings need more than just the air, food, and water we consume. Abraham Maslow refers to those other human needs as self-esteem and self-actualization. Patrick Lencioni calls it our need to do something relevant, something that makes a difference in the lives of others. A sense of purpose drives us and provides the energy to get us out of bed and to work.

  There are some days when life gets the best of us, when our personal circumstances are particularly difficult, and work can be a potent distraction that allows us to recover our equilibrium and gain perspective. My sister, whose personal life is full up with high demand from two special-needs sons, finds that her job at a hospital gives her a break of eight or more hours a day from the rigors of her home situation.

- **Work offers relationships.** Even when we struggle with co-workers, having them around forces us to engage. Human beings crave belonging and connection, and for many people work is a primary way to form relationships. Work reduces isolation, and when we see colleagues, hear about their

"

Work gives us a way to contribute.

lives, and engage with them in shared tasks and accomplishments, we feel good. Even when they're not our best friends, we look forward to seeing them and being with them.

- **Work stimulates our brains.** Humans like to think. Having to think stimulates us. Jobs that demand creativity, innovation, problem solving, and exploration challenge us. Once we're done with school, work is the logical place for us to bring and use our powerful brains.

- **Work connects to identity.** Work is an important dimension of my identity, intertwined with my roles of mother, wife, friend, daughter, athlete, baker, etc. My sense of myself is strongly connected to the work that I do, both paid and unpaid, that makes a difference to someone. It brings me comfort, at the end of the day, to know that I have used my assets to do something good or helpful. This is true for most people.

Let's give a thumbs up to the sanctity of work.

In Chapter 11 we'll explore the last element for creating a Bravespace workplace, Lever V – How: The Soft Stuff and Being Real.

ACTIONS FOR CREATING BRAVESPACE WORKPLACES
Meaning and Context

For Leaders or Business Owners

- Spend time to think about and write down why your business exists, beyond the marketing tagline. Why does the world need you? What difference does your organization make?

- Challenge every leader on your team to connect the purpose of your organization to every person who works for them.

- Connect your customers' experiences to your employees' experiences. They feed off each other and are two sides of the same coin.

- Learn how to share context in both directions – with your board, shareholders, and investors on the one hand, and your employees at all levels on the other. Learn how to share it simply and clearly.

- Think about your why: Why are you in your role? Why did you start this company? Tell the story repeatedly.

For Employees

- Take time to understand why you choose to work at this place. What difference does it make?

- Consider the reason that your organization exists. Ask yourself if you can support this reason and how.

- Know why you work, beyond the paycheck.
- Talk about the good stuff that work brings you.

For HR or People Development (if they exist in your company)

- Make sure that new hires are vibrantly on board so that they understand from the beginning why the company exists and what their part in it is.
- Emphasize *Why?* in recruiting practices and documents.
- Challenge yourself to meet the needs of your employees beyond your role in compliance and administration.
- Train managers at all levels to connect meaning to their leadership practices.

Chapter 11

๛

Lever V – How
The Soft Stuff and Being Real

*Emotional labor is not invisible work or unpaid
chores. It's when a job requires you to show or
hide emotions – flight crews staying calm, teachers
showing passion, nurses showing compassion. It's as
vital as physical and cognitive labor.*

— Adam Grant

*A*UTHENTIC HAS BECOME A WIDELY OVERUSED WORD
today. I've seen it used to train customer service reps
who plaster fake smiles on their faces and ask, "How's your
day going?" when they couldn't care less. Authentic is added to descriptions of furniture, clothes, and hotel rooms to
connote *original* when the product is really a newly made
copy of something original. And it's used to train leaders
at all levels how to act with their employees in ways that
garner trust and partnership.

I find it ironic that another retail term for *authentic* is *distressed*, as in "distressed denim" and "distressed cabinet," which are used as selling points to show that the item has some fraying around the edges. It doesn't look freshly minted, right off the factory floor, which makes it appear to us more friendly, warm, and "real." When human beings are authentic (real) as Margery Williams (1922) said so poignantly in the children's book classic *The Velveteen Rabbit*, they're easier to love. The problem is that the overuse of the word has strained its meaning, making interactions at times palpably artificial. Like the made-up things around us, we sometimes mimic others in a way that, despite our intentions, allows others to sense that we're not being our authentic selves.

Being Real

An essential element of Bravespace workplaces is the presence of authentic expressions of humanity and of human nature. *Remember, a Bravespace workplace is one in which people can show up as they are, both worthy and flawed, and do great things together.* Rather than being carte blanche for people to wear their bathrobes to work and blurt out their thoughts at the expense of others, being real at work means something completely different. What being real means is unique to each one of us. We know it in our gut when someone is showing up authentically, and we can sense when someone is faking it. No amount of reading,

BEING REAL

"Real isn't how you are made," said the Skin Horse. "It's a thing that happens to you. When a child loves you for a long, long time, not just to play with, but REALLY loves you, then you become Real."

"Does it hurt?" asked the Rabbit.

"Sometimes," said the Skin Horse, for he was always truthful. "When you are Real you don't mind being hurt."

"Does it happen all at once, like being wound up," he asked, "or bit by bit?"

"It doesn't happen all at once," said the Skin Horse. "You become. It takes a long time. That's why it doesn't happen often to people who break easily, or have sharp edges, or who have to be carefully kept. Generally, by the time you are Real, most of your hair has been loved off, and your eyes drop out and you get loose in the joints and very shabby. But these things don't matter at all, because once you are Real you can't be ugly, except to people who don't understand."

— Margery Williams, *The Velveteen Rabbit*

training, or degrees can guarantee that we'll capably be true and real with others at work. The work of being real with one another at work requires, rather than piling on new skills, stripping away the protective layers that keep our feelings, opinions, and tensions hidden. Decades of

"

We know it in our gut when someone is showing up authentically, and we can sense when someone is faking it. No amount of reading, training, or degrees can guarantee that we'll capably be true and real with others at work.

politically correct, ingrained ways of being at work must be put aside in order to discover the unique, true, and honest story that we bring to work every day. There are seven practices for being real that work:

- **Walk your talk.** The fastest way to erode trust is to espouse one thing and do another. We tune in to one another at work based on what we see done, not what's promised. A client of mine was the general manager of a company. He told his team that family needs come first, so they should prioritize their families when it came to work-related impacts such as overtime and weekend interruptions. During a regularly scheduled meeting one Monday, one of the directors asked the GM if he had expected a response to his email, sent at 5 a.m. on the Sunday prior to the meeting? The director had seen the email when he came to work, hadn't really read it, and worried that his boss expected an answer by the time they met Monday. The subtext of their conversation was, "You say you want us to prioritize family, but you consistently work evenings and weekends. This tells me that you expect me to as well, despite what you say." To their credit, this was a fruitful conversation. The GM openly owned his own 24/7 working style and acknowledged that his direct reports might interpret his behavior as contradicting his words. They agreed that there were times when it was essential to go the extra mile, but that these instances should be exceptions and not the rule given what they valued.

- **Name the ugly, scary, and hard.** The single most common behavioral problem I see in workplaces is the reluctance of people to dig into unsavory, challenging, and painful conversations. There are resources to help people navigate conflict, give feedback, and have difficult but crucial conversations, but instead we often avoid those difficult interactions. There are a host of reasons why we don't have the hard conversations we need to: fear, insecurity, concern about hurting another, identity, shame, perfectionism, positional authority, fear of recrimination, risk, and more. But here's the thing: a Bravespace workplace is built on honesty, honesty that's kind and compassionate. For nearly a century, management practice has scrubbed feelings out of workplaces as if they're dirty. But Bravespace workplaces are built upon the recognition that feelings are essential elements of the workplace that we must work through together.

I had a client once who was preparing to announce layoffs to the employees who remained. Originally his talk was composed mostly of data and numbers that gave the context of his decisions. But the reality was that he was sad and hurt that the company had to lay off people, including some of his friends, in order to survive. His decision to start his presentation by sharing his own sadness at the layoffs had the opposite effect of what he expected. He was worried about appearing weak, but his tenderness and tears were reassuring to others. They felt sad and lost as well, and by naming the dark part of the process he cleared the way for everyone to understand why the changes had to happen and what was necessary going forward. We must always tell the truth about the hard stuff, with care, with kindness, and with compassion.

- **You're the leader, you go first.** Employees copy leaders. They tune in to what their leader is doing to determine what they should be doing. Remember that whenever you act.

  Years ago, I sailed across the Pacific with a small crew. I was on night watch, in the middle of the Pacific Ocean, when we hit something. I alerted the crew and the captain, who came topside. My pulse and my panic were racing. "Have we damaged the hull?" "Should I lower the sails?" "Where's the life raft?" When I saw the captain, I noticed his calm demeanor. He quietly listened. He called down below to the others, "Does anyone see or hear water below?" He adjusted the sails to get us on course and off the accidental jibe we had done. I felt my panic subside. I firmly held the wheel and started going through the checklist in my head. Without being aware of it, and without any direction from the captain, I had begun to internalize his reactions and demeanor and make them my own. He knew more than I did about things that go bump in the night in the wild open ocean, and his calm moves informed mine. As leaders, we must go first toward creating a Bravespace workplace. What we do, others will copy.

- **Remember, there are no guarantees.** People ask me how they can trust other people if they have no proof of trustworthiness. They're looking for a guarantee, wondering, "If I lean into you, open my heart to you, show you my unformed ideas, share my input with you, will I be safe? Or will something bad happen?" We're alert for the things that threaten our feelings of security and our identity: Will you insult me? Diminish me? Will you tell me no? Will you keep my

"

At work, just as in life, there's no guarantee. We may feel hurt, diminished, insulted, or alienated at work; we may even be fired. These are the risks of living.

"

Most of us come to work wanting one thing: to do a good job and to be worthy.

secret? Will you tell me the truth? Will you leave me? Will this hurt?

At work, just as in life, there's no guarantee. We may feel hurt, diminished, insulted, or alienated at work; we may even be fired. These are the risks of living. Every day we face rejection and loneliness as we take the risk to make friends and to love. We form connection and meaning at work through the presence and practice of vulnerability, which Brené Brown describes as uncertainty, risk, and emotional exposure. At work our sense of self-worth is most vulnerable – "Am I worthy and competent here?"

Most of us come to work wanting one thing: to do a good job and to be worthy. As Brown (2012) says, "Vulnerability is not weakness, and the uncertainty, risk, and emotional exposure we face every day are not optional. Our only choice is a question of engagement. Our willingness to own and engage with our vulnerability determines the depth of our courage and the clarity of our purpose; the level to which we protect ourselves from being vulnerable is a measure of our fear and disconnection." There are no guarantees that our courage in contributing to a Bravespace workplace will be rewarded, but the only alternative is to opt out and work independently and in isolation. When we work with others there's no guarantee that it will all work out, but we must show up anyway. The hard parts of work make the sweet parts even sweeter.

- **Remember that it all made sense at the time.** In the context of Bravespace workplaces, it's easy to look in the rearview mirror and find blame, shame, or recrimination for the mistakes we or others have made. We tell ourselves things like "They never should've hired him," or "This will never work," or "How did they mess it up *this* badly?" When we do this, we waste time and effort assigning blame, rather than using that time and effort to together create solutions for moving forward. My favorite mantra, "It all made sense at the time," profoundly eases the feelings of blame and recrimination we feel when we look at our past actions.

    Every day, people make decisions in the best way they know how according to their present knowledge. We don't know what we don't know. We proceed toward action without surety or completeness. If we remember that a decision of the past made sense at the time (for the people who

##

❝

Remember that it all made sense at the time.

made it), we spend less time obsessing on our past actions and are more able to move forward with grace and forgiveness.

- **Use self-compassion as evidence of empathy.** When I make a mistake, the things I say in the privacy of my own mind are astounding. I would never say them to a friend, or to an employee:

  "How could you be so stupid?"

  "What on earth were you thinking?"

  "You shouldn't be surprised this turned out badly, you are a loser."

  "What made you think you could do this?"

  When I look at my own imperfections, I often become negative, hostile, judgmental, and shaming toward myself. It doesn't help me, and it doesn't help others. When we treat leaders as people who can and should do things perfectly, we risk creating disconnection and eroding trust. In our deficit-oriented, results-focused business culture, accountability often looks like this kind of self-recrimination.

When leaders focus on their weaknesses, and verbally abuse themselves for being less than perfect, they demonstrate to those around them that they lack compassion and empathy. It's the human condition to learn from our mistakes, so more mistakes mean more learning. Exhibiting self-compassion to those around us indicates that we have an accurate sense of self as both worthy and flawed and that we see mistakes, including our own, as opportunities to learn. We model empathy and move on. What helps others is to know that we're capable of having empathy for difficulty, including our own, and we believe that a solution or remediation is possible.

- **Own your sh****. I was interviewing clients for a structure project recently. The group of fifteen employees told me that their boss was having a toxic impact on the whole team. I shared the anonymous feedback with the boss, who became visibly upset. He said, "How can these people afford the time to whine and complain about me to you? This just goes to show you – they're incompetent and lazy." Hmmmm. Surely, the employee group contributed to the team's eroded trust, but when fifteen people report to a neutral third party that the boss's mean and negative behavior is demoralizing them, it's wise to at least be curious about it. Better yet, own it.

What I wished for this leader was that he had recognized his employees' pain as real and that he had empathized. Then he could have become genuinely interested in how others saw him and why they said those things. The perception that others had about his impact was terrific information about what changes he could and should make to his leadership practice. Had the leader owned up to his impact, recognizing that his positive intention hadn't reached its audience, he might have shown his team that he wanted to lead them and that he was willing to learn.

Some of the ways he could have done this include being curious about his own reaction to their feedback. He could have asked questions such as, "Why am I so negative?" "Why am I disappointed?"

"

People make companies great, which means that the great companies of tomorrow are the ones that will attract people to work for and with them, and that the quality of those workplaces will encourage people to flourish.

"

We can't have the positives without the negatives, which means that leaders of the Bravespace workplaces of tomorrow will spend time, energy, effort, and resources to tend to the beautiful "soft stuff" that their people bring to work every day.

"What needs to happen with the group?" If he had asked himself reflective questions such as these, he could have learned about himself, which would have helped him to lead differently and to positively impact his company.

The Soft Stuff

Often when I describe to people what I do, they call it "the soft stuff," which implies work that focuses on people but is disconnected from the business. There is a tendency in business to focus on getting a measurable return on investment in people and organizational development. I get it – we want to know if the effort and expense make a difference. The fact is, it's hard, if not impossible, to measure whether our efforts with regard to people have the impact we want, where we want it. As a CEO once said to me, "I can't measure in dollars and cents whether our work on culture here has made our company better single-handedly, but I can sure tell you that it has had a positive impact qualitatively." When we do the right thing for people, we know it and it feels right. When we don't, it doesn't.

People make companies great, which means that the great companies of tomorrow are the ones that will attract people to work for and with them, and that the quality of those workplaces will encourage people to flourish. That quality will be maintained in these same Bravespace workplaces so that the people who work there continue to thrive.

The soft stuff of a workplace fit for human life inspires people to choose to come to work, and to stay once they get there. These workers contribute wisdom, energy, ideas, experience, talent, courage, and authority. They also bring to the workplace their imperfect humanity, their egos, their past wounds, their fears, their insecurities, and their complex needs. We can't have the positives without the negatives, which means that leaders of the Bravespace workplaces of tomorrow will spend time, energy, effort, and resources to tend to the beautiful "soft stuff" that their people bring to work every day.

In the next chapter, we'll discuss how to use these five levers for creating Bravespace workplaces by examining specific actions while we imagine a future where people bring their best to work.

ACTIONS FOR CREATING BRAVESPACE WORKPLACES
The Soft Stuff and Being Real

For Leaders or Business Owners

- Be authentic, don't just act authentic. Take time to understand your motivations, your gifts, your strengths, and your weaknesses. Tell the truth, with grace and kindness.

- Ask for feedback (often) about your impact. Ask yourself if you're having the impact you want.

- Challenge your leaders at all levels to deepen their practice of both vulnerability and courage. Go first with both in ways that your next-level leaders see and experience.

- Take the time to define the results you hope to get, but don't get too hung up on measuring ROI.

- Walk your talk.

For Employees

- Pay attention to whether leaders at all levels are authentic and work to get to know them.

- Study your own feelings, needs, and fears, and learn from your emotions.

- Bring your open heart to leadership and to your teammates so that your ideas and opinions are heard and seen. This doesn't mean that your ideas will always be implemented, but the company will know where you stand and may learn from your input.

- Remember that perfection is unachievable. This will help you to be more empathetic for the imperfections of others and to recover quickly when you misstep.

For HR or People Development (if they exist in your company)

- Make sure that your company's values and guiding principles ae grounded in behavior and match its actual people practices.

- Hold the mirror up to leaders to help them hold themselves and each other accountable for walking their talk. Do pulse surveys, culture surveys, or focus groups to hear from employees how they experience their managers.

- Ensure that policies are driven by values, so that when people are asked to do something by you it makes sense to them.

- Sharpen your skills at modeling authenticity and honesty. Have hard conversations swiftly and with a positive end in mind.

PART IV

Act Now!

Chapter 12

❧

Where to Start?

Great projects start out feeling like buildings. There are architects, materials, staff, rigid timelines, permits, engineers, a structure. It works or it doesn't. Build something that doesn't fall down. On time.

But in fact, great projects, like great careers and relationships that last, are gardens. They are tended, they shift, they grow. They endure over time, gaining a personality and reflecting their environment. When something dies or fades away, we prune, replant and grow again.

Perfection and polish aren't nearly as important as good light, good drainage and a passionate gardener.

By all means, build. But don't finish. Don't walk away.

Here we grow.

— Seth Godin

"

Spend time getting your head behind the notion that the greatness of your company depends on the people in it.

Now that the idea of Bravespace workplaces has been introduced and defined, it's time to get started on the specific actions you can take using the tools we've covered so far.

Let's look at a CEO with whom I recently worked. He was struggling with the internal dynamics of his company despite incredibly fast financial success. His employees were feeling tired and burned out. His leadership team needed to step away from the details to focus on the future, but they didn't know how. He had two senior leaders whom employees feared. He himself was worried about the toll on his marriage and home life. I told him that I thought I could help. "Great," he said. "Will it be complex?" "Nope, not complex," I said, "but not easy either."

It can be hard to know where to start when it comes to creating a workplace that truly brings out the best in everyone who works there. In my 30-plus years of experience consulting with companies of all types, here are the top ten behaviors to start with:

1. **Adopt a people-centered mindset.** Spend time getting your head behind the notion that the greatness of your company depends on the people in it. Being people-centered doesn't mean your company exists so that your people can be happy; it means designing your workspace – the physical and felt environment of your organization – to encourage people to thrive. Thriving people bring all their talents to benefit your company.

2. **Bring flexibility to your approach.** There's no one right way to create a Bravespace workplace. Your way will be unique to you and will depend on the nature of your business, your style of leading, and the unique alchemy of your workforce. Be flexible with what others have tried, and don't be afraid to

"

There's no one right way to create a Bravespace workplace. Your way will be unique to you and will depend on the nature of your business, your style of leading, and the unique alchemy of your workforce.

"

Consciously choose to see beyond profit to other indicators that your company is doing well.

customize your approach based on your values and priorities. Stick with what we know people need from work (revisit Chapter 4), and stay focused on fulfilling those needs.

3. **Involve others.** Leaders in the best companies I've worked with take the necessary time and effort to get input and ideas from everyone who works there. This doesn't mean that they make decisions by consensus, the tediousness of which can grind productivity to a crawl, but rather that leaders at all levels make it a priority to ask people what they think, listen to their responses, and communicate openly and freely in both directions. Open involvement increases buy-in, which increases participation, which increases ownership. Open involvement makes everyone at your organization accountable, not just you.

4. **See the benefit beyond.** Your top priority will remain the efficacy and performance of your company, but remember that your company's profit depends on its overall health. The communities

in which you operate should be enhanced by the presence of your organization, the environment in which you operate and the resources you use should be responsibly cared for, and the people who work for you should feel that they're better people as a result of working for your organization. Consciously choose to see beyond profit to other indicators that your company is doing well.

5. **Address leaders first.** Every employee at every level knows the company through their direct manager. Period. This means that even if you're the best CEO, general manager, executive director, or business owner in the history of the world, if one of your leaders is a tyrant, an abuser, or just a negative influence, your employees will not thrive. In Bravespace workplaces, time, energy, resources, and conversation are invested in the art and science of leading well. Nothing matters more. Leadership is not for the faint of heart, and advanced degrees and years of experience don't necessarily make a great leader. Know when you have a great leader, one who

"

Every employee at every level knows the company through their direct manager. Period.

inspires loyalty, fosters esteem, and brings out the best in your people. Develop those leaders and keep them.

6. **Remember that life is work.** We work for many reasons, but no matter what our motivations are, our work is part of our lives. It matters to us and it impacts our human development, our view of the world, and our ability to thrive at home and in our communities. The life that your employees live outside of work shapes and defines the life

"

The life that your employees live outside of work shapes and defines the life they bring to work, so don't pretend that there's a wall between the two. The people, activities, and circumstances your employees encounter away from your workplace are essential to what they bring into the workspace, so talk to them about those things.

"

Start somewhere, anywhere,
and keep at it. Small changes
have a huge impact on the way
your employees experience
your organization.

they bring to work, so don't pretend that there's a
wall between the two. The people, activities, and
circumstances your employees encounter away from
your workplace are essential to what they bring into
the workspace, so talk to them about those things.

7. **Start with small changes.** It doesn't take a radical
   change to have a positive impact and bring
   your company closer to becoming a Bravespace
   workplace. There's no need for a wholesale makeover
   or herculean consulting resources. Start somewhere,
   anywhere, and keep at it. Small changes have a
   huge impact on the way your employees experience
   your organization. Small, effective changes are far
   preferable to big, romantic, programmatic changes
   that will fail for lack of bandwidth.

8. **Listen to understand.** Having almost finished
   reading *Bravespace Workplace*, you may feel that
   you know where to start and what to do. Good for

"

When you listen to your leaders, to front-line employees, and to customers, you add nuance, detail, and clarity to the ideas you have about what to do.

you! Go out and talk to people in your organization about your ideas and hear what they think. Really listen. As the owner, CEO, general manager, or executive director, it's difficult for you to see your organization in a neutral way: your position limits your perspective. When you listen to your leaders, to front-line employees, and to customers, you add nuance, detail, and clarity to the ideas you have about what to do.

9. **Align head and heart.** Remember that emotion is part of your brain, too, and that your emotional states are a powerful source of information to help you and others make decisions and lead. Whether you have an MBA, 30 years in your industry, or just a killer technology to bring to market, focus on your heart skills. Doing so will grow your capacity to engage with others, to create meaningful connection, and to inspire followership more than anything

else you might try. We are drawn to vulnerability in others, so bravely show up.

10. **Walk your talk.** People who work for you will read the memos, come to the all-hands meetings, and adhere to the policies. But more than anything else, they'll watch and absorb what you, and the leaders you hire, do day in and day out. Everything, from how you run a meeting to what hours you work, communicates information to your employees about what you value. This, in turn, shapes their point of view about whether your company is one in which they can learn, grow, and thrive. Make your actions conscious, ask about the impact you have, and do what you say you will do. Your employees are watching.

The work of becoming a Bravespace workplace is all about bringing out the absolute best in the human beings who

❝

Remember that emotion is part of your brain, too, and that your emotional states are a powerful source of information to help you and others make decisions and lead.

work in them, despite our imperfect and complex human motivations, habits, needs, and issues. Bravespace workplaces are people-centered because their leaders deeply understand that it is people who make all the positive things happen at work. If you want your company to become a Bravespace workplace, start at any of the elements we've looked at in this book. Start with courage, because even when you don't know the answer, there is a way forward. Start with heart, because it's what draws people to you and your company. Start with faith, because while you, too, are imperfect, you want to lead your organization, and what you do matters.

Just start.

"

Everything, from how you run a meeting to what hours you work, communicates information to your employees about what you value.

Epilogue

૭

ICAN PRACTICALLY TASTE WHAT IT WOULD BE LIKE if every employer decided to become a Bravespace workplace. I've seen enough organizations achieve it that I know in my bones that it's possible. I am motivated by my deepseated hope for my children and yours that we, the business owners, the leaders, and the entrepreneurs, will foster a quiet but potent revolution that turns the tide of job misery for once and for all.

When this happens, people will work with energy and optimism, not every day of course, but most days. Work itself, at all stages of life, will be viewed as central to our wellbeing, as important as rest and health, instead of simply as the drudgery we face on the road to retirement. Through work we'll achieve meaning because we know the impact of our effort. At work people will find critical connections with other human beings, connections that reduce their isolation and loneliness.

Work will no longer erode and suffocate the health of our beloved families and friends because we're overwhelmed and overworked. Instead, work will enliven and enrich families of all types. Everyone will feel free to make choices that support their families, whether it's taking leave after a child is born or adopted, caring for elders, working flexible hours, or having virtual meetings. Organizations will include insider groups and outsider groups at all levels, so that across the identifiers of race, gender, sexual orientation, and more, there will be equity and inclusion. Men and women will make equal pay for equal work.

Work will be a place where mistakes happen on the road to learning, and where shame is replaced by compassion and worthiness. At work we'll play sometimes and we'll value rest as essential to productivity. Hard conversations will happen in the Bravespace workplaces of tomorrow, driven by the belief that conflict is essential to partnership, and we'll be both clear and kind.

Leaders of tomorrow's Bravespace workplaces will show up, be real, and lead by example and integrity. They'll model the common values and vision that benefit all employees so that together we remember why we do what we do and how we want to work together.

Bravespace workplaces of tomorrow will be profitable, but not at the expense of the environment or the communities in which they operate.

With the knowledge that people are what make companies great, Bravespace workplaces of tomorrow will be healthy and safe places for people to co-exist. In these places, our children, and theirs, will be able to bring their gifts, their ideas, their talent, their wisdom, and their experience

forward even as they bring their quirks, their imperfections, and their needs. They'll be welcomed whether they
are insiders or outsiders, for their talents and gifts and for
the ways they're different and for the ways they're alike.

In the Bravespace workplaces of tomorrow, work will be
the place we go to activate, enliven, and tenderly support
the complicated humans that we are so that we can bring
all of ourselves to work every day. It will be a place where
we create great things together, learn, connect, and contribute.

Notes

৶

Agarwal, Dimple, Josh Bersin, Gaurav Lahiri, Jeff Schwartz, and Erica Volini. 2018. *Deloitte Insights: The Rise of the Social Enterprise.* https://www2.deloitte.com/content/dam/insights/us/articles/HCTrends2018/2018-HCtrends_Rise-of-the-social-enterprise.pdf.

Amy Edmondson. 1999. "Psychological Safety and Learning Behavior in Work Teams." *Administrative Science Quarterly* 44 (2): 350–83.

Aristotle. 2011. *Aristotle's Nicomachean Ethics.* Translated by Robert C. Bartlett and Susan D. Collins. Chicago: The University of Chicago Press.

Barnhart, Gordon. 2018. *Center for Heroic Leadership.* http://www.heroicleaders.com.

Bartlett, Jamie. 2017. "Silicon Valley's Wealthy Elite Have Made Social Inequality Worse." *The Spectator* (August 12). https://www.spectator.co.uk/2017/08/silicon-valleys-wealthy-elite-have-made-social-inequality-worse/.

Bennis, Warren. 2009. *On Becoming A Leader,* 4th Edition. New York: Basic Books.

Bloom, Nicholas. 2017. "Corporations in the Age of Inequality." *Harvard Business Review* (March 21). https://hbr.org/2017/03/corporations-in-the-age-of-inequality.

Bloomberg. 2018. "Where Have All the Public Companies Gone?" (April 9). https://www.bloomberg.com/view/articles/2018-04-09/where-have-all-the-u-s-public-companies-gone.

Brodzinksi, Pawel. 2014. "The Fallacy of the Ideal Team Size." *Software Project Management* (January 28). http://brodzinski.com/2014/01/ideal-team-size-fallacy.html.

Brown, Brené. 2010. *The Gifts of Imperfection: Let Go of Who You Think You're Supposed to Be and Embrace Who You Are.* Center City, MN: Hazelden Publishing.

Brown, Brené. 2012. *Daring Greatly: How the Courage to Be Vulnerable Transforms the Way We Live, Love, Parent, and Lead.* New York: Avery.

Brown, Brené. 2018. *Dare to Lead.* New York: Penguin Books.

Buckley, Patricia, and Daniel Bachman. 2017. "Meet the U.S. Workforce of the Future: Older, More Diverse, and More Educated." *Deloitte Review* (July 31). https://www2.deloitte.com/insights/us/en/deloitte-review/issue-21/meet-the-us-workforce-of-the-future.html.

Bureau of Labor Statistics. 2018. "BLS Data Viewer." https://beta.bls.gov/dataViewer/view/timeseries/CES0500000002.

Burlingham, Bo. 2016. *Small Giants: Companies That Choose to Be Great Instead of Big.* New York: Portfolio.

Cappelli, Peter, and Anna Tavis. 2016. "The Performance Management Revolution." *Harvard Business Review* (October). https://hbr.org/2016/10/the-performance-management-revolution.

Carrick, Moe, and Cammie Dunaway. 2017. *Fit Matters: How to Love Your Job.* Palmyra, VA: Maven House.

Cilluffo, Anthony and D'Vera Cohn. 2017. "10 Demographic Trends Shaping the U.S. and the World in 2017." *FactTank: News in the Numbers* (April 27). Pew Research Center. http://www.pewresearch.org/fact-tank/2017/04/27/10-demographic-trends-shaping-the-u-s-and-the-world-in-2017/.

Day, Matt. 2018. "Take a Look Inside Amazon's Spheres as They Get Set to Open." *The Seattle Times* (January 26). https://www.seattletimes.com/business/amazon/take-a-look-inside-amazons-spheres-as-they-get-set-for-next-weeks-opening/.

Drum, Kevin. 2017. "You Will Lose Your Job to a Robot – and Sooner than You Think." *Mother Jones* (November/December). https://www.motherjones.com/politics/2017/10/you-will-lose-your-job-to-a-robot-and-sooner-than-you-think/.

Drysdale, Carla, ed. 2018. World Economic Situation and Prospects 2018. United Nations. https://www.un.org/development/desa/dpad/wp-content/uploads/sites/45/publication/WESP2018_Full_Web-1.pdf.

Friedman, George. 2016. "3 Reasons Brits Voted for Brexit," *Forbes* (July 5). https://www.forbes.com/sites/johnmauldin/2016/07/05/3-reasons-brits-voted-for-brexit/#5de9a3f11f9d.

Gallup. 2013. *State of the American Workplace: Employee Engagement Insights for U.S. Business Leaders.* https://www.gallup.com/services/176708/state-american-workplace.aspx.

Gallup. 2017a. *State of the American Workplace.* https://www.gallup.com/workplace/238085/state-american-workplace-report-2017.aspx.

Gallup. 2017b. *State of the Global Workplace.* https://www.gallup.com/workplace/238079/state-global-workplace-2017.aspx.

Gerzema, John, and Michael D'Antonio. 2013. *The Athena Doctrine: How Women (and the Men Who Think Like Them) Will Rule the Future.* San Francisco: Jossey-Bass.

Google. "Guide: Understand Team Effectiveness." *Re:Work.* https://rework.withgoogle.com/guides/understanding-team-effectiveness/steps/introduction/.

Hardoon, Deborah. 2015. *Wealth: Having It All and Wanting More.* Oxfam Issue Briefing (January). https://d1tn3vj7xz9fdh.cloudfront.net/s3fs-public/file_attachments/ib-wealth-having-all-wanting-more-190115-en.pdf.

Heffernan, Margaret. 2015. *Beyond Measure: The Big Impact of Small Changes.* New York: Simon and Schuster, TED Books.

Hilbrecht, Margo, Bryan Smale, and Steven E. Mock. 2014. "Highway to Health? Commute Time and Well-Being among Canadian Adults." *World Leisure Journal* 56 (2): 151–63. https://doi.org/10.1080/16078055.2014.903723.

Jaques, Elliott. 1990. "In Praise of Hierarchy," *Harvard Business Review* (January 1). https://hbr.org/1990/01/in-praise-of-hierarchy.

Kan, Michelle, Gad Levanon, Allen Li, and Rebecca L. Ray. 2018. "Job Satisfaction 2018: A Tighter Labor Market Leads to Higher Job Satisfaction (Executive Summary)." Conference Board. https://www.conference-board.org/publications/publicationdetail.cfm?publicationid=8121.

Lencioni, Patrick. 2002. *The Five Dysfunctions of a Team*. San Francisco: Jossey-Bass.

Levy, Jonathan. 2014. "Accounting for Profit and the History of Capital." *Critical Historical Studies* 1, No. 2 (Fall), 171–214.

Maslow, Abraham H. 1943. "A Theory of Human Motivation," *Psychological Review* 50 (4): 370–96.

McKinsey Global Institute. 2018. "How Will Automation Affect Jobs, Skills, and Wages?" (March). https://www.mckinsey.com/featured-insights/future-of-work/how-will-automation-affect-jobs-skills-and-wages.

McQueen, Nina. 2018. "Workplace Culture Trends: The Key to Hiring (and Keeping) Top Talent in 2018." LinkedIn Blog (June 26).

Mejia, Zameena. 2018. "Nearly 9 Out of 10 Millennials Would Consider Taking a Pay Cut to Get This." CNBC (June 28).

Merriam-Webster. 2018a. S.v. "happiness." accessed November 9, 2018, https://www.merriam-webster.com/dictionary/happiness.

Merriam-Webster. 2018b. S.v. "thrive." accessed September 29, 2018, https://www.merriam-webster.com/dictionary/thrive.

Nunberg, Geoff. 2016. "Goodbye Jobs, Hello 'Gigs': How One Word Sums Up a New Economic Reality." *National Public Radio* (January 11). http://www.npr.org/2016/01/11/460698077/goodbye-jobs-hello-gigs-nunbergs-word-of-the-year-sums-up-a-new-economic-reality.

Pachauri, R.K., and L.A. Meyer, eds. 2014. *Climate Change 2014: Synthesis Report*. Contribution of Working Groups I, II and III to the Fifth Assessment Report of the Intergovernmental Panel on Climate Change. Geneva, Switzerland: IPCC.

Pew Research Center. 2018. "Mobile Fact Sheet." Pew Research Center: Internet & Technology (February 5). http://www.pewinternet.org/fact-sheet/mobile/.

Pfeffer, Jeffrey. 2018. *Dying for a Paycheck.* New York: Harper Collins.

Pimentel, Diego, Alejo Vázquez, Iñigo Macías Aymar, and Max Lawson. 2018. *Reward Work, Not Wealth.* Oxfam Issue Briefing (January). https://d1tn3vj7xz9fdh.cloudfront.net/s3fs-public/file_attachments/bp-reward-work-not-wealth-220118-en.pdf.

Posner, Barry, and Jim Kouzes. 2010. *The Truth About Leadership: The No-Fads, Heart-of-the-Matter Facts You Need to Know.* San Francisco: Jossey-Bass.

Poswolsky, Adam Smiley. 2015. "What Millennial Employees Really Want." *Fast Company* (June 4). https://www.fastcompany.com/3046989/what-millennial-employees-really-want.

Raworth, Kate. 2017. *Doughnut Economics.* New York: Random House Business.

Rosen, Rebecca J. 2011. "Project Classroom: Transforming Our Schools for the Future." *The Atlantic* (August 29). http://www.theatlantic.com/technology/archive/2011/08/project-classroom-transforming-our-schools-for-the-future/244182/.

Rozovsky, Julia. 2015. "The Five Keys to a Successful Google Team." *Re:Work* (November 17). Google. https://rework.withgoogle.com/blog/five-keys-to-a-successful-google-team/.

Schein, Edgar H. 1985. *Organizational Culture and Leadership.* San Francisco: Jossey-Bass.

Schulte, Brigid. 2014. *Overwhelmed: Work, Love, and Play When No One Has the Time.* New York: Sarah Crichton Books.

Schwartz, Barry. 2015. *Why We Work.* New York: Simon and Schuster, TED Books.

Sinek, Simon. 2009. *Start with Why.* New York: Simon and Schuster, TED Books.

Small Business Administration. 2012. "Frequently Asked Questions." SBA Office of Advocacy.

Smith, Emily Esfahani. 2013. "There's More to Life Than Being Happy." *The Atlantic* (January 9).

Smith Major, Virginia, Katherine J. Klein, and Mark G. Ehrhart. 2002. "Work Time, Work Interference with Family, and Psychological Distress." *Journal of Applied Psychology* 87 (3): 427–36.

Spicer, André, and Carl Cederström. 2015. "The Research We've Ignored About Happiness at Work," *Harvard Business Review* (July 21). https://hbr.org/2015/07/the-research-weve-ignored-about-happiness-at-work.

Stafford, Coe Leta. 2018. "What Is Design Thinking?" IDEO U. https://www.ideou.com/blogs/inspiration/what-is-design-thinking.

Talbot, Danielle, and Jon Billsberry. 2007. "Employee Fit and Misfit: Two Ends of the Same Spectrum?" 1st Global e-Conference on Fit, The Open University.

Tuckman, B. W. 1965. "Developmental Sequence in Small Groups." *Psychological Bulletin, 63* (6), 384–99.

Turing, A. M. 1937. "On Computable Numbers, with an Application to the Entscheidungsproblem." *Proceedings of the London Mathematical Society* 2, 42 (1), 230–65,

Turing, A. M. 1950. "Computing Machinery and Intelligence." *Mind* 49: 433–60.

Vaillant, George E. 2012. *Triumphs of Experience*. Cambridge, MA: Belknap Press.

Vingerhoets, Ad. 2013. *Why Only Humans Weep*. Oxford, U.K.: Oxford University Press.

Weber, Max. 1958. *The Protestant Ethic and the Spirit of Capitalism*. Translated by Talcott Parsons. New York: Charles Scribner's Sons.

Wheatley, Margaret J. 2002. "It's an Interconnected World," *Shambhala Sun* (April). https://margaretwheatley.com/articles/interconnected.html.

Williams, Margery. 1922. *The Velveteen Rabbit*. New York: George H. Doran Company.

Woolley, Anita, and Thomas W. Malone. 2011. "Defend Your Research: What Makes a Team Smarter? More Women." *Harvard Business Review* (June 1). https://hbr.org/2011/06/defend-your-research-what-makes-a-team-smarter-more-women.

Index

჻

INDEX

INDEX

INDEX

About the Author

๑

Mom, daughter, gardener, wife, ex-wife, adventurer, entrepreneur, and consultant, Moe Carrick believes that people make organizations great. Companies large and small are routinely brought to their knees by the "soft stuff" of people problems – as anyone knows who has tried, this work is hard. As a facilitator, protagonist, consultant, entrepreneur, author, employer, and relentless optimist, Moe believes that people can and should thrive at work, and that when they do, organizations succeed. With over 30 years of work in organizations on issues of partnership, leadership, inclusion, strategy and culture, Moe believes that rigorous self-awareness, courage, honest dialogue, active involvement, and empathy are fundamentals to building full partnerships based on trust and curiosity. As a white, U.S.-born, heterosexual woman, Moe strives to use her privilege with grace to surface assumptions that interfere with teams and to explore systemic patterns.

Moe holds a master's degree in organizational development, is a Certified Daring Way™/Dare to Lead™ Facilitator, a coach, and an administrator of a variety of tools in her trade. She is also a senior consultant with White Men as Full Diversity Partners (WMFDP), the market leader in including white men in the critical conversations required to sustain truly inclusive cultures.

Moe is passionate about the role work plays in creating meaning for our lives and in the role business can play as a force for good. She is a regular blogger on topics related to people at work and is a contributor to *Conscious Company* magazine. Maven House Press released her first book, the bestseller *Fit Matters: How to Love Your Job*, with co-author Cammie Dunaway, in 2017.